Children with Special Needs

Michael Luxford

Children with Special Needs

Anthroposophic Press

First published in 1994 by Anthroposophic Press
and Floris Books

Published by Anthroposophic Press
RR4 Box 94 A1, Hudson, NY 12534

Front cover photograph by Thomas Horan
Back cover photograph by Leslie Lawson

ISBN 0-88010-381-7

Printed in Great Britain
by Redwood Books,
Trowbridge, Wiltshire

Contents

1. Normality and abnormality

An encounter

'Hello Peter.'

Peter does not reply but looks at his parents. I hold out my hand and he takes it with a hesitant response. Peter has arrived with his parents for an interview as he may come as a student here, to this college and therapeutic community based on the curative educational ideas of Rudolf Steiner (1861-1925). He visited three years ago but went elsewhere in the meantime. Now his parents have returned with him. He has been living at home for the past year following a period at another 'special' college. Although he is twenty years old, he is immature and could be fifteen or sixteen years old according to his appearance and in other ways he could be only seven.

A twenty-year-old young man who is immature, can't understand the use of money, has limited reading or writing ability, can't tell the time and still needs help in remembering to change his clothes and to wash himself. Soon all the support of the authorities will cease and he may have to stay at home all day. The family lives on a farm, he can roam about and do easy jobs for his father. His mother says that if he would be at home all day he would drive her 'up the wall' because he hangs around her, talks constantly and is always thinking of what to say next. He has no real friends other than some local younger children with whom he is quite happy to play.

His early history tells of a long, difficult birth, and as a baby he would not sleep. He never crawled, only sat up with help at two years of age and walked at four. By then he had some

words but it wasn't until he was seven or eight that he had
speech sufficient for basic communication. Over the years he
has had a lot of help and he has enough speech for day-to-day
needs and for keeping talking all day.

Peter's mother was in tears as she told of his birth and early
years. His father was sure that Peter needed to make more
progress than can happen even with five days of care at a local
day-centre and at home. 'He needs motivating and bringing on
and if it doesn't happen soon, by his middle twenties it will be
too late. He needs a peer group experience.'

It may seem strange to begin a book on the subject of curative education with the example of a twenty-year-old young
man. However, my response to meeting Peter was that he
would have needed curative education from an early age and by
the latest his mid-teens. If this had happened he might well not
have been paying this second visit and, according to his father,
standing on the edge of a future burdened by immaturity and
limited social abilities.

The question is: what could curative education have offered
him which might have and may still make a difference to his
life? We cannot answer the question at this stage but will
approach it through a general survey of historical and present
day curative educational work and by then we may see how
someone like Peter could be helped. We can begin by considering one of the basic issues related to curative education, namely
terminology.

Normality and abnormality

Rudolf Steiner did not give a clear-cut definition of curative
education but he did say what was required if anyone wished
to practise it. Basic to this is the need to develop an understanding of normality in relation to abnormality. In the first lecture
of his course to would-be curative educators he said:

> In some corner of the life of soul of every human being
> lurks a quality or tendency that would commonly be

Rudolf Steiner
(1861-1925)

called abnormal. It may be no more than a slight tendency to flights of thought, or an incapacity to place the
words at the right intervals in speaking, so that either the
words fall over each other or else the listener could go
for a walk between them. Irregularities of this kind —
and they are to be found also in the life of will and of
feeling — can be noticed, to some slight degree, in the
majority of human beings.[1]

Today, in the so-called developed world such an idea would
be considered the norm but we can note that the above remark

was made in 1924. We may take this as a philosophical issue
but it is obvious that progress in the care and education of
children who are developmentally unusual depends on the ideas
and ideals which inspire therapeutic practices. Fundamental to
this care and education is the attitude of the educator towards
those he is to help.

Rudolf Steiner's words from further on in this opening
lecture lead today's reader from an idea to a starting point for
curative practice:

> The only possible grounds we can have for speaking of
> the normality or abnormality of the child's life of soul,
> or indeed of the life of soul of any human being, is that
> we have in mind something that is normal in the sense
> of being average. At present there is really no other
> criterion. That is why the conclusions people come to are
> so very confused. When they have in this way ascer-
> tained the existence of 'abnormality,' they begin to do —
> heavens knows what — believing they are thereby help-
> ing to get rid of the abnormality, while all the time they
> are driving out a fragment of genius.

Here the human being is presented from an opposite
perspective. Firstly, the normal person was described in whom
could be found abnormal tendencies. Now the so-called
abnormal person is seen as someone who may possess qualities
of genius. This seeming contradiction warns us to beware of
generalizations over normality and abnormality but also
encourages us to develop unprejudiced observations and to be
open for new ideas. '... we must refrain from jumping to
conclusions, and simply *look at things as they are*. What have
we actually before us in the human being?'

Curative education concerns itself with the needs of the
developing child and youngster where they are significantly
different from the norm as to require special attention. It
follows from the above passages that it is essential for the
curative educator to acquire a developing understanding of the
human being.

*Karl König
(1902-66)*

Karl König (1902-66) the Austrian doctor and pupil of Rudolf Steiner who founded the Camphill Movement for Curative Education, stressed the all-encompassing nature of curative education. In the opening chapter of his book *Being Human,* after having asked the question 'What is curative education?' he says that a single answer cannot be given. He then suggests that curative education is a practical art to which there are no set rules.

We must always be innovative and creative in relating to each child or adult, otherwise it does not work. That is

the one side of the coin. On the other hand if curative
education were nothing more than a practical art, none of
us would be good curative educators. We also need a
practical knowledge to constantly replenish our creative
activity. It should not mean simply being able to name
and describe each child's condition — names are just so
many empty words. The crucial element in curative
education diagnostics is the effort we make to thoroughly
understand whatever confronts us in the individual.[2]

What has been said so far leads us to identify three fundamental necessities if curative education is to be effective. These
are:

— Knowledge of the human being.
— Observation, particularly of abnormalities.
— Understanding, which can lead to a therapeutic approach.

This threefold key opens the door to curative education and
therapy, but before we try to turn this key we should consider
the origins of curative education, how it was forged and shaped.

The historical background

In Great Britain in 1978 a report was presented to Parliament
entitled 'Special Educational Needs: A report of the Committee
of Enquiry into the Education of Handicapped Children and
Young People.'[3] This report was chaired by the now Dame
Mary Warnock and reflects a significant moment in the development of special education in Britain. It can be taken as an
example as to how historical thinking has progressed in a
western European country. The kind of thinking contained in
what is generally known as the Warnock Report and which
underpinned the 1981 Education Act does not stand in isolation
from other ways of approach in the rest of Europe, Scandinavia
and North America. The Warnock Report represented a significant effort of a so-called civilized democratic society to apply

itself to the needs of the 'handicapped' child or youngster. We must bear in mind that even in the 1990s a large proportion of the world's nations have only basic policy outlines for addressing these kinds of need and may well have little or no actual provision.

Special education in Britain began in the eighteenth century with the founding of schools for the blind and deaf. In the mid-nineteenth century schools for physically handicapped children were also being founded, whilst so-called mentally handicapped children were still placed in workhouses and asylums. Words like 'imbecile,' 'idiot' and 'defective' were in common usage.

In England, the Foster Education Act of 1870 and a similar one in Scotland, The Education Scotland Act of 1872, opened the way for special provision for these mentally 'defective' children:

In the 1890s a concerted effort was made to change the system of education for 'feeble-minded' and 'defective' children and to address the question as to how far these children could be educated in normal school settings.

In 1924 the Mental Deficiency Committee, the Wood Committee, asserted that there were 105,000 children currently requiring special education and about ten per cent of all children were failing to make progress in ordinary schools. The Wood Committee concluded that:

> If the majority of children for whom these schools are intended are, *ex hypothesi,* to lead the lives of ordinary citizens, with no shadow of a 'certificate' and all that that implies to handicap their careers, the schools must be brought into closer relation with the Public Elementary School System and presented to parents not as something both distinct and humiliating but as a helpful variation of the ordinary school.

The Warnock Report remarks that it still took many years before the unqualified right of mentally handicapped children to education was recognized. The report became the basis for the further development of special education in Britain. Two aspects stand out. Firstly, its emphasis on providing combined schooling where the categorization of children into handicapped and normal children would end:

> Categorization perpetuates the sharp distinction between two groups of children — the handicapped and the non-handicapped — and it is this distinction which we are determined, as far as possible, to eliminate.

Secondly, one hundred and sixteen years after the Lunacy (Scotland) Act of 1862, the Warnock Report recommended the following:

> We consider that it would be preferable to move away from the term 'educationally sub-normal' or in Scotland 'mentally handicapped,' terms which can unnecessarily stigmatize a child not only in school, but when he comes to seek employment. We recommend that the term 'children with learning difficulties' should be used in future to describe both those children who are currently categorized as educationally sub-normal and those with educational difficulties who are often at present the concern of remedial services.

In Holland, by way of comparison, a similar process of enlightenment happened in the nineteenth century. In 1841 the first Act was passed, the Act on Insanity *(Krankzinnigenwet)*. Prior to this the so called mentally defective were hardly distinguished from the insane. They were nursed in convents, hospitals or even jails in the cases of aggressive behaviour.

In 1855 the first home with schooling for 'feeble-minded' children was founded. From this time onwards many such homes were started by private persons and societies. The first school was known as a Day School for Minor Idiots *(Dag-school voor minderjarige idioten)*.

In 1884 a fourth Act of Insanity was passed which regulated these homes and institutions, but to this day the clear distinction between the psychiatrically ill person and the child or person

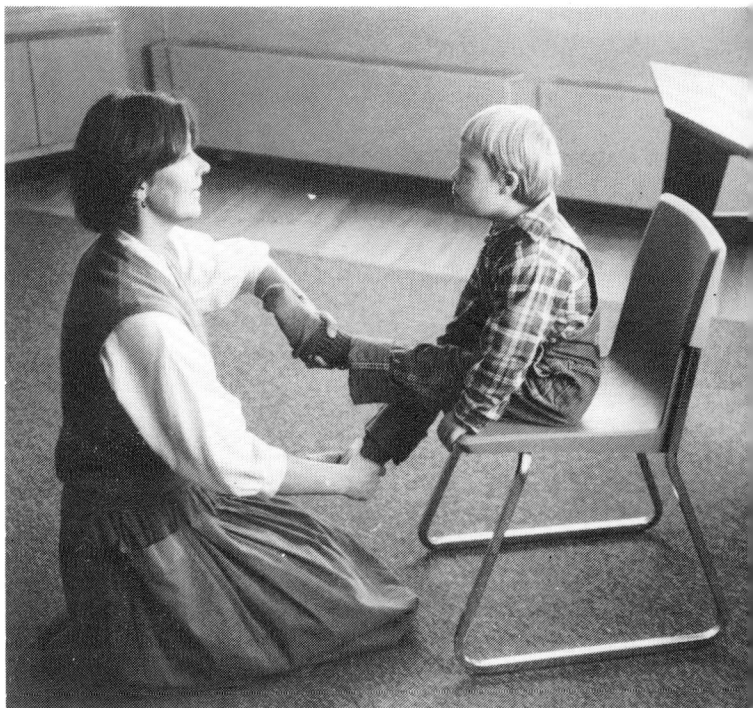

Using specific movements as therapy.

who is developmentally different has yet to be made. However, the special and curative educational movement has developed through its own impetus.

Recently the Dutch Legislative Assembly has been discussing the inclusion of a special section to a new Act. The Bill on Special Admission in Mental Homes (B.O.P.Z.) *(Wetsontwerp Bijzondere Opneming in Psychiatrische Ziekenhuizen)* should state that the 'feeble-minded' be treated as a separate category in society having special needs.

Comparative terminology

In Holland before 1900 the following terms were in use: *dol*
(mad), *onwijs* (fool), *onnozel* (innocent), *arm van geest* (poor
in mind). Later these names were superseded by *debiel* (backward), *imbeciel* (imbecile), *mongool* (Down's syndrome). Today
the terms used are: *zwakzinnig* (feeble-minded), *geestelijk
gehandicapt* (mentally handicapped), *verstandelijk gehandicapt*
(intellectually handicapped) and *mensen met mogelijkheden*
(people with potentialities).

In Germany, the term *geistige Behinderung* corresponds to
the English mentally handicapped. *Lernbehinderung* corresponds
to learning difficulties. In the nineteenth century *Debilität,
Imbezillität* and *Idiotie* differentiated differing degrees of mental
handicaps. To date there has yet to emerge a comparable term
to the English 'special needs' or the Dutch, 'person with potentialities.'

In France the term used is *les déficients intellectuels,* the
intellectually deficient. In America, it is 'mental retardation' or
'developmental disabilities' and in South Africa 'persons with
mental handicap.'

A time of change

In the period described above tremendous changes have taken
place in what we call current thinking. What was an acceptable
idea in the 1890s is totally unacceptable today. Yet the term
curative education remains virtually unknown in the English-
speaking world, even to the professional practitioners within so-
called special education. The word derives from *Heilpädagogik*
which is the term used in Germany to describe the approach
used in helping children with special needs. In this word two
concepts, 'healing' and 'education,' are combined. The act of
healing is often taken to have medical or religious connotations,
as in the healings of Christ who not only acts with divine

intervention but also cures medically described conditions such as blindness, the palsy, derangements and so on.

The word 'education' derives from the Latin *educere* which means 'to lead forth.' How different the world would be if education started from the premise that every child possesses inherent spiritual gifts and capacities and the task of the teacher is to lead these forth and make appropriate space for the unfolding of the inherent faculties of the child. Instead we have the frantic pressing *into* the child of intellectual and practical capacities which set standards against which we measure success and normality. The child is caught between the two pressures: those of its own capacities and gifts, and the demands of twentieth century economic necessity.

One of the main tasks of curative education is to get away from solely assessing the capacities of the child and to add to it the fostering of the unique qualities possessed by the child and young person. It is not good enough to aim for integration of these individuals at some low functioning level of the social-economic ladder. Instead, we are challenged to discover different values from those which predominate in our age, which appears to be obsessed with the glorification of success.

2. The history of curative education

Steiner as tutor

As already mentioned Rudolf Steiner asked the group of young curative educators to whom he was speaking in 1924 to 'refrain from jumping to conclusions, and simply *look at things as they are.* What have we actually before us in the human being?'

This approach must have been in the forefront of his mind when, as a young student in his twenties, Steiner lived for six years with a family in Vienna as the tutor to their four children. One of these, Otto, a hydrocephalic large-headed youngster, was hardly able to read and write, and had great difficulties with any kind of learning. Steiner's task with these children involved him not only in the usual educational tasks but presented him with the challenge of educating Otto. He was regarded as a problem child and Rudolf Steiner wrote of him:

> His thinking was slow and dull. Even the slightest
> mental exertion produced headache, lowering of vitality,
> pallor and a state of mind that caused anxiety. After I
> had come to know the child, I formed the opinion that
> the sort of education required by such a bodily and
> mental organism must be one that would awaken dorm-
> ant faculties. I had to find access to a soul which was, as
> it were, in a sleeping state and must gradually be enabled
> to gain mastery over the bodily manifestations. In a
> certain sense one had first to draw the soul into the
> body. I was thoroughly convinced that the boy actually
> had great mental capacities, though they were hidden.

This educational task became for me a source from
which I learnt a great deal. Through the method of
teaching which I had to employ there opened to my view
the association between the element of soul and spirit in
man and the bodily element. In this way I went through
a real course of study in physiology and psychology. I
became aware that education and instruction must become an art that has its foundation in a knowledge of the
human being.[4]

With Rudolf Steiner's help, Otto not only began to learn but
completed his secondary education and entered Medical School,
eventually qualifying as a doctor. We have to imagine Rudolf
Steiner setting out to discover methods through which such a
sensitive child, prone to various weaknesses, was able to make
exceptional progress. Although having no specific training,
Rudolf Steiner was able to develop insights which, once applied
to the healing of this boy, enabled him to enter a profession
instead of being what everyone would have expected, a disabled
and incapacitated individual. We can say that Rudolf Steiner's
achievement with Otto was possible because he was able to
discover the therapeutic insights which were needed to help this
particular human being.

Success of this kind calls for an intense involvement and
interest in the other person. This kind of interest appears to be
the common factor in all of the pioneers of what is termed curative education. In the lives of each of the following personalities the encounter with a child is the starting point. The choice
of personalities has already been made by Karl König in his
monograph *Mignon; A Tentative History of Curative Education*
and is included here because the author believes Karl König's
choice is original, understandable and remains relevant.[5]

The pioneering spirits

In the simpler if harsh world of the eighteenth century the
French doctor, Jean Itard (1775–1838) encountered the 'Wild

Jean Itard
(1775-1838)

Edouard Séguin
(1812-80)

Boy of Aveyron.' This boy had grown up separated from other human beings in the forests of the south of France. Itard responded to this child with the utmost enthusiasm and interest, attempting to help him and lead him into civilization. This attempt was not completely successful but despite remaining intellectually simple, the Wild Boy of Aveyron was able to find a place in society.

Edouard Séguin (1812–80) was a pupil of Itard and worked in the Hospital Bicêtre in Paris where a department for mentally disturbed children had been started. Séguin is known for his attempts at the description of these children. Even if today a title like *The Moral, Hygienic and Educational Treatment of Idiots* would be found offensive, we can still recognize the beginnings of a curative educational effort — identifying the needs of children and finding ways to understand their situation and seeking remedies.

The Swiss doctor, Hans Jacob Guggenbühl (1816–63) whilst still a medical student had encountered a 'cretin' girl and was so moved that he vowed to 'dedicate his life to the relief of this misery and to suffer defeat rather than abandon this cause of humanity.' Within five years of this meeting, Guggenbühl opened his institution for treatment of 'cretins' on the Abendberg near Interlaken. Here Guggenbühl developed special methods in teaching and in general therapeutic measures, developing models of village settlements for those suffering from cretinism.

Each of these three doctors — Itard, Séguin and Guggenbühl — were prompted by their encounters with 'special children' to discover new methods of treatment and education. They were pioneers not only because they wrote fundamental treatises on what they had discovered but because they had responded to these children directly and purposefully. They were doctors who became educators.

Heinrich Pestalozzi (1746–1827) is known as the guiding spirit and founder of the Pestalozzi Villages which continue to give shelter to thousands of homeless children. He lived in the aftermath of the French Revolution witnessing the momentous events happening across Europe at this time. He realized that the children who had been cast adrift and abandoned had sunk

Hans Jacob
Guggenbühl
(1816-63)

into a state of poverty and suffering both of soul and body. His attempt was to provide a home and help to some of these children. He wrote in 1775:

> On admission, most of the children were in a state that was the miserable outcome of utterly neglecting all that is human quality. Many arrived with deeply-rooted scabies so that they could hardly walk, many with eruptions on their heads and many with sores crawling with vermin. Many were emaciated like skeletons, sallow and grinning, their eyes wide with fear and their brows knitted in wrinkles of care and distrust. Some were bold and impertinent, accustomed to begging, to hypocrisy and to all falsehood. Others were subdued by suffering, docile but suspicious, afraid and without love.

Heinrich Pestalozzi
(1746-1827)

He witnessed the changes which took place in these children once the opportunity for human decency became available to them. In his letters we can grasp what means he used to treat these children:

> From morning until night I was practically alone in their midst. All the good done to their bodies and souls came from my hand. All help, all relief from suffering, every lesson that they received came directly from me. My hand lay upon their hands, my eyes rested upon their eyes, my tears flowed with their tears and my smile accompanied their smile. They were lifted above this world; they were with me and I with them. Their soup was my soup, their drink my drink.

In 1841 a young Italian by the name of Giovanni Bosco (1815–88), was ordained into the Catholic priesthood. He had spent his childhood and youth among the local urchins and ruffians and discovered in himself an ability to calm and alter the lives of these children. He decided to dedicate his pastoral care to their needs and within two years he created in Turin a string of havens for an estimated seven hundred abandoned and impoverished youngsters.

As his work developed Don Bosco, the name by which he is known, succeeded in lifting these children out of their depraved and crime-ridden life into an ordered, purposeful existence. This did not happen without opposition and his goodness had to endure persecution. In 1859 he founded the Order of the Salesians and by the time of his death the work of the Order had spread throughout Europe and South America, running schools and workshops.

Thomas Weihs, a writer on Don Bosco, says of him:

> Giovanni Bosco left no system or method of education behind, yet he guided hundreds and thousands of children away from depravity and crime towards true humanity. His motto was *Praevenire Non Reprimere* — to prevent not to punish. He was a man who matured without losing the child in himself and for this reason, he had access to the souls of the most fallen children, and was able to appeal to the innate pureness and spiritual nearness in them, going before them as an example.[6]

In the East End of London in 1866 a young medical student and preacher, Thomas John Barnardo (1845–1905), was led by a little boy called Jim Jarvis through the dark streets of London and witnessed for himself the sight of hundreds of children sleeping in the open, without protection and dressed only in rags. Deeply moved by this experience he founded the East End Juvenile Mission in order to help these destitute children. He acquired houses for them to live in and began schools, teaching them and providing employment training. He said of his children:

*Don Bosco
(1815-88)*

They are not fair, nor are they kingly yet in spite of their
rags, their dirt, their crippled limbs, their wounds, their
bruises, their sores and their scars, these little pilgrims
are ambassadors of the King. There is always something
beautiful in these little ones, however disfigured they
may be with sin and suffering. Something which fills us
with reverence for children.[7]

It is said that by his death sixty thousand children had been
helped back into society and to their own humanity.

Itard, Séguin, Guggenbühl, Pestalozzi, Don Bosco and Thomas
Barnardo — these were some of the founders of curative education, each one having experienced in a child something which
called them to be more than doctor, priest, teacher or social
worker. The child seemed to show them possibilities for their
own lives which were as yet unknown and in the service
of which, not only the one child, but hundreds, even thousands,

Thomas John Barnado (1845-1905)

Child sleeping rough in London, 1876.

were helped and healed. It was as if the life of the curative
educator was meant to become one of healing. In the will to
act, to do something, compassion was transformed into powerful deeds of love.

Steiner's influence

Despite his achievement with the boy Otto, Rudolf Steiner
never entered into substantial curative educational work, though
its origin and development as a practical expression of anthroposophy is inconceivable without his involvement. Anthroposophy is the term used to describe the method of research and
scientific investigation inaugurated by Rudolf Steiner. It derives
from the Greek *anthropos* meaning man and *sophia* wisdom
and can be said to encompass the development of knowledge of
the whole human being not only in his bodily and psychological
condition but also in his spiritual capacity.

It was after the First World War that two young teachers,
Siegfried Pickert and Franz Löffler, took up posts in a large
Children's Home in Jena, Switzerland and came to know
Albrecht Strohschein, a student of psychology.

In 1924 these three approached Rudolf Steiner for advice as
they were starting a new Curative Home at the 'Lauenstein.'
They knew of anthroposophy and were sure that Rudolf Steiner
could help them. As soon as the Lauenstein had taken in its
first children he visited them, saw the children and gave de-
tailed diagnostic indications for treatment, both medical and
therapeutic. Following this visit Rudolf Steiner gave a course of
twelve lectures in Dornach, Switzerland. These lectures provide
the basic approach and orientation for anthroposophical curative
education.

At first, the three individuals concerned, Pickert, Löffler and
Strohschein had been uncertain as to what they wanted to
achieve. Strohschein says:

> In fact, we had none of us meant to go in for curative
> education. Destiny had connected us to the problems of

The founders of curative education: Werner Pache, Franz Löffler, Ita Wegman, Siegfried Pickert, Albert Strohschein, 1924.

mentally backward children and we had simply sought for anthroposophical light in a sphere where we saw others helpless.[8]

During the visit to the Lauenstein, Rudolf Steiner challenged them to break through to new therapeutic possibilities by means of which children and young people, like the young Viennese Otto, would be able to reveal and express what was otherwise in danger of remaining hidden.

The home which Pickert and his friends were to take over had existed as a 'Home for Pathological and Epileptic Children.' Rudolf Steiner objected to this terminology and suggested instead the description 'Curative and Educational Institute for Children in Need of Care of the Soul.' He said 'We must choose a name that does not stamp the children immediately.' The usual term today has become Children in Need of Special Care.

Albrecht Strohschein remarked:

Now I slowly realized for the first time that 'care of the soul' was something belonging to all education, which everyone might be called upon to practise; there was therefore nothing in it to separate our children from others.

We can already conclude that one expected outcome of curative educational effort should be a significant change for the better in the quality and potentiality of life for the child or youngster with special needs. The child's life should become different and be relieved of some of the burden which has been created by the remark some parents have heard at the birth or early examination of their child 'you cannot do anything for him.' How many mothers and fathers have responded with a determined 'yes, we can' and as parent or teacher have led the child to unfold and flower in ways inconceivable and mysterious to the pragmatic thinker. Curative education describes an approach which many parents have discovered for themselves. Many teachers have achieved the same for their pupils as did Pestalozzi, Don Bosco and Barnardo.

Curative education addresses the needs of the child or young person who requires special care and education. In certain aspects it is in harmony with general methods of education applied to the child who we say has 'learning difficulties.' In other ways curative education, based on anthroposophy, differs from what we usually understand as special education. Our purpose is to outline the reasons for this divergence and to attempt to describe anthroposophical curative education philosophically and practically.

3. Child development

Looking into the eyes of a new-born baby you see how far
away, how profound and universal that child is, and at the same
time it looks deep into you. Focussing is not yet possible,
physical needs are simple and powerful. There is an atmosphere
of wonder and joy which only the hard of heart would deny is
heavenly and pervaded by innocence.

It takes time for the first stages of child development to
begin: the moving gaze, the look, the smile, the grasping hand,
the raising of the head and suddenly, sitting up. Already much
has changed by the time the baby has become an infant, crawl-
ing and pulling itself up and finally, triumphantly standing up
by the chair or table. One day, a special day, the child will take
its first walking step. This is the first major milestone.

During this time the baby has been weaned from the
mother's or other milk and is now able to eat food from the
earth, preferably food which is not too heavy; gentle, nurturing
foods, fruit, vegetables and grains.

Already sounds and cries have become recognizable and
eventually words will be heard which will become meaningful
alongside other words. Objects will be named and this active
toddler who has been watched and cared for will begin to
speak. Overt movements established in the body and limbs
prepare the way for more subtle movements focussed in the
organ of speech.

The ability to speak, to recognize objects and events in the
world, leads to meaningful expressions, statements and questions. The child takes in the world through its senses and distils
it within itself, making a statement or expression, indicating the
beginning of thinking.

Alongside the archetypal milestones of walking, speaking

and the germination of thinking the child becomes a determined 'three year old' who may possess a surprisingly powerful self-will. The awareness of self in a child is not the same as it is later but marks its arrival into its own contextual world. From then on it is an 'I,' a Richard, Fiona, John. You become mum, dad and so on. The child will cast off the nappy and other supports to babyhood. Having lain at the breast and in the arms it will climb its way into the high chair and eventually into a grown-up's chair, into shoes instead of slippers, into coats instead of blankets and shawls.

To come thus far, to become a determined toddler, reaching out or lying next to you listening to a story at bedtime, is to have won through the first stage of life on the way into the world.

The developing child

The young child's life is immersed in imitation. It takes in the world and transforms its impressions through imitation into play. I remember watching an uncle of mine paint a garage door. I watched his every movement, the sanding, cleaning and painting, every detail. For weeks afterwards I would repaint this door with a bucket of water and an old brush I had found. It was the same with the coalman who filled the coal shed. I would create sacks and lorries and coal mines in the garden and the miners with their black faces. Anything and everything was possible in the playground of my imagination which created new worlds each day in the fifty square metres of our garden. Impressions were translated into action by the power and faculty of imitation.

Naturally it is healthy if the child can continue in the imitative world as long as possible as the imaginative way of learning is an inherent faculty in the child. This adventurous and interesting phase needs the support of home, letting the child play but still in a protected, confined area. Gradually this will change and the time to meet other children in the playgroup will arrive. Other children with their wishes and determination

Awe and wonder.

Life and energy.

have to be encountered, play has to become socialized and early learning leads into schooling.

Early childhood and play, influenced and enhanced by the power of imagination, can be characterized as a time of doing. Achievements are gained through the will of the child. If the milestones and their inherent faculties have been acquired then a healthy, active, interested child makes its way through the doors of school and finds its first teacher.

The child goes to school with apprehension but also with expectation, looking for new experiences. In addition to meeting other children in the playground there is the wider world provided by the lessons, the mythological, the legendary and finally the historical world. The world is discovered in its number, colour, word, material, fluid, geographical, astronomical, political, social, racial, chemical, biological, poetic, warlike, religious nature and so on. All these will be revealed and if the teacher has the right attitude the child will take in everything with devotion and wonder as if a closed door is being opened inch by inch. The acquisition of reading and writing not only provides access to education and learning through literature but enables the soul to express itself.

Potentially this is a wonderful phase, the time of the opening of the child to the world and to the faculty of learning through interest. The teacher becomes the admired, loved presence in the child's life who has been given the right to know. 'My teacher said, so there.' The child is harmonious, the boys and girls are not so dissimilar physically and it is usually a time of health once childhood illnesses are left behind. There are moments of inwardness when the experience of oneself becomes stronger.

The entry into the teenage years is marked by what Rudolf Steiner called 'earth maturity.' This is an interesting expression denoting a deeper stage of integration into earthly life for the individual soul. At this time a significant moment of further integration takes place when a clearer contrast appears between the male and female qualities, both physically and psychologically.

Adolescence, from the Latin *adolescere,* means 'to grow into manhood' and denotes the stronger emergence of individualized experience. It describes the psychological aspect of the young person which develops along with the physical changes introduced by puberty. Erik Erikson describes three stages within this phase:

Puberty   Identity Seeking   Coping

With puberty the youngster has to accept the 'falling' into earth maturity and the changes which take place. Increased self-awareness, the changing appearance and whether one's appearance is liked or disliked have to be encountered.

The resistance to family and the struggle to find one's own

Scientific experiments help to explain the mysteries of everyday life and aid integration into the world.

feet, one's own standpoint, begins at a time when independence and intellectualization of thinking, one's own cleverness, has only just been discovered. Idealization begins as well as concern for the world. The young person arrives at the thought: 'Well, life can't always be perfect. I don't think I am perfect but I can make something out of myself. I will just have to get on with it.' Eventually they will know what they want to do with their life and will set out to achieve it, being prepared for failure or success. Thinking enables the youngster to arrive at balanced judgments and to cope with varying emotions and to accept others as independent persons to whom they have to relate as friends, as colleagues and maybe as husband or wife.

The milestones and characteristic features of child development up to early adulthood are the measure against which the question is asked: 'Is this child well, and progressing in growth and development?' When any of the milestones or other features fail to appear or appear too soon or too late we become worried. The mother may say: 'I realized after a few months that my baby did not look at me;' or 'My child did not make any effort to sit up until it was nearly nine months. I knew something was wrong.'

Pathways in childhood experience

The survey of child development in its predetermined features provides the basic framework for what we may regard as normal and abnormal development. When features appear which significantly diverge from the norm we are justified in speaking of abnormal development. However, we must remember that the idea of a norm is an abstraction as in reality we are only concerned with an average within the multicoloured landscape of childhood. Instead of separating out the abnormal into categories of children we can point to the variety of experiences to which the individual child may be subject. There is not one journey but many journeys which the child may make. We can now turn our attention to a number of different children and try to experience their journeys and encounters.

A smile that opens doors: Down's syndrome

During a class trip to Greece to view the ancient temple sites, a group of children with a wide mixture of special needs and their teachers had to negotiate with a variety of shopkeepers, garage owners and so on who were not particularly helpful because the teachers could not speak the language. For the first few days these encounters were fraught with anxiety until it was noticed that if Marie, a pupil with Down's syndrome, entered a shop ahead of the rest the otherwise uninterested proprietor seemed to cheer up and become more helpful. Her ability to make an immediate contact with other people changed these encounters into moments of fun. The teachers tried to not misuse Marie but it was a great help and a source of some amusement to see this little ambassador of sunshine push through the door because she wanted to be the first to say 'Hello.' She was entirely innocent and successful despite having a complete ignorance of the language in common with the rest of the party.

If you look at the faces and figures of any group of children in a playground, all have nose, ears, mouth and so on but none the less the impression is of a group of individuals. Compared with this differentiation of features, Down's syndrome gives rise to similarities in facial and physiological characteristics which for many people epitomize the 'handicapped child.' These features bridge racial types and create a group of people where a form and personality are held closely in common. In meeting such children you cannot help feeling they are brothers and sisters though without family ties.

Each has an abnormal chromosome layout, having forty-seven instead of the usual forty-six. Normally the extra chromosome is linked to the twenty-first pair of chromosomes though there are other forms where it may be attached to another one or be deleted. This is the one aspect, the chromosome abnormality. The other is the observation that these children retain into birth and afterwards an appearance which is common to all of us in the second month of embryological development. The Down's syndrome child holds onto this time and retains its impress into later life. Therefore these children

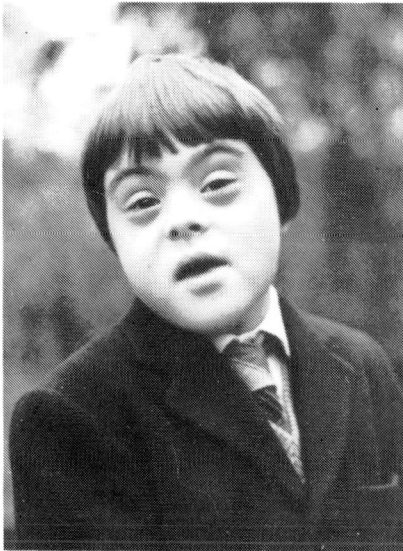

Two children, both with Down's syndrome.

do not enter into the usual process of differentiation into individuality and are held back developmentally within babyhood or childhood. The mystery of the integration of the soul into its human form is clearly seen in the child who carries the destiny of Down's syndrome.

Early milestones — sitting, standing, walking, toilet training and the acquisition of speech — are mostly late and it may be that adequate speech will be hard to achieve as also will intellectual thinking. Psychologically these children live in a world of imagination and imitation and because of this are open, friendly and make the world into their home. They are innocent and only rarely show guile. Like small children they can be naughty and suffer if they are discovered or reprimanded.

Their delicate constitution, often having a heart condition and being easily prone to colds and minor illnesses, calls forth a protective gesture but they must also be helped to enter into education and become citizens of the world. Their development must be carefully nurtured if we are to help them to be part of society, not only for their own sakes but for the sake of society itself. We should not be overcome by excessive sympathy and compassion for such children as this will hinder us in finding the purpose of their journey for themselves and for the world. Today the general picture, as presented above, of the placid and friendly child must also include the different challenge met in the more capable Down's syndrome youngster who may show difficult behaviour and even aggression.

Waiting in the wings: childhood autism
Since the middle of this century we have become increasingly aware of a particular group of children who have come to be described as autistic — a term deriving from the Greek *autos* meaning 'self' and implying being alone with oneself. This condition is distinguished from other related conditions such as Asperger syndrome which, though having similar features, describes children who are not so aloof as the autistic child but show obsessive preoccupation with particular thoughts and patterns of thought.

Descriptions of autistic children, both physically and

behaviourally, show similarities in the same way as with Down's syndrome. The mother's experience of a lack of eye contact with her new born child may not immediately lead her to the idea that something is amiss. She may be puzzled and a little concerned but as time goes on she realizes that a warmth of relationship between the child and herself and the child to the world seems to be lacking.

Usually, by the third year it will be apparent that there is a contact disturbance in which the child appears to be cut off from its surroundings. This will manifest in various ways, through their look, their flat personality in which there may be sudden outbursts of screaming and aggression, in particular mannerisms which may have developed, in hand movements or in holding the head to one side for long periods of time. Next to the general indifference to people and surroundings there may be forms of excessive interest often related to the ordering

---

A. Onset before 30 months of age.

B. Pervasive lack of responsiveness to other people (autism).

C. Gross deficits in language development.

D. If speech is present, peculiar speech patterns such as immediate and delayed echolalia, metaphorical language, pronominal reversal.

E. Bizarre responses to various aspects of the environment: e.g., resistance to change, peculiar interest in or attachments to animate or inanimate objects.

F. Absence of delusions, hallucinations, loosening of associations, and incoherence, as in schizophrenia.

Criteria for infantile autism.[9]

of objects in particular ways. Play is lacking in the usual sense as imagination and imitation are overtaken by fixation. Such children will often react badly to their arranged world being disturbed and parents can be forced to accept imposed living conditions in order to keep the peace. It is well known that these children can have islands of advanced intellectual and artistic ability.

I remember an encounter with such a child whom I had known for some time. I was sitting on a bench at the bottom of a long flight of stairs when he came running down. He came up to me, took hold of my hands, looked at me briefly with his beautiful blue eyes and hopped up onto my lap. Taking my arms and wrapping them round him, he leant back against me. He sat for a long time and whereas with another child it would have been a moment of warmth and fondness, perhaps leading to a little conversation about school or something else, with him

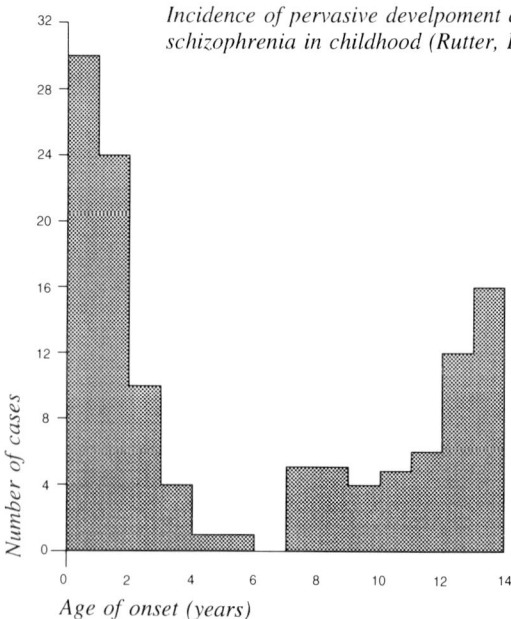

Incidence of pervasive develpoment disorders and schizophrenia in childhood (Rutter, BMA, 1974).

I felt myself become completely empty and my initial joy in this seemingly sudden outbreak of affection changed into a feeling of sadness at the distance which separated the child and myself. On other occasions this boy could become enraged by some minor interference into his world and would react by biting deeply into the arm or leg of the one who had offended.

The Down's syndrome child loves the world and flows easily along with it. By contrast these withdrawn children are reluctant to say 'Yes' and usually find it impossible to accept themselves as being part of the world, addressing themselves as 'You' or 'John.' This feature is known as pronominal reversal. It is difficult for them to find access to the crucially important experience of knowing oneself as 'I.' It is another person, the world, which calls us 'You' or 'John.' Only by experiencing oneself as 'within oneself' can you know that you are an 'I.' Hence childhood autism is bound up with the problematics of acceptance of the world and self.

The title of Bruno Bettelheim's book *The Empty Fortress* encapsulates the dilemma present in finding an adequate therapeutic approach.[10] We may indeed feel affronted by the human being who holds back from involvement, appears to build a fortress against this complicated, problematical world of ours. To adopt a Buddha-like stance to life is impossible and to erect almost unassailable walls is infuriating. Yet, if one tries to scale the walls and push down the doors one only forces the soul of the child to retreat even further. Ways of helping the child have to be found if they are to accept the world and others, but not through approaching the child head-on.

There are other major developmental disorders in childhood which manifest in fundamental personality disturbances, distorted perception and response. Autism shows particular features and must be differentiated from other forms of disturbance as in the later appearing childhood schizophrenia or psychosis.

Reaching out hesitantly: cerebral palsy
If we observe a baby after its first few months it is already attempting to turn its head in the direction of its mother. This possibility of exerting control over the head contrasts with the

still instinctive, uncoordinated movements of the limbs. By six
months control will have descended to the lower trunk and the
child will then have managed to sit. Eventually this step will
lead to it standing and walking by the time of its first birthday.
We observe here the descent of a controlling factor from the
head into the body and out into the limbs. Balance is being
established as the child becomes a toddler, raising itself up onto
its small feet and chubby legs with its arms and hands out-
stretched in a magical moment of steadiness. The delightful,
dreamy small child who is clumsy and always knocking into
tables and falling down needs someone, usually the mother, to
keep an eye on him. Some small children are just like this and
certain features of cerebral palsy are quite normal at a certain
stage. There are children who take a long time to achieve
bodily and spatial integration.

In cases of cerebral palsy we are concerned with disturbances of primary movement development — cerebral palsy
being an umbrella term for a number of conditions: *spasticity,*
where there is stiffness and loss of control in the limbs and
muscular spasm; *athetosis,* characterized by involuntary movements with lack of control over the whole body including facial
control; *ataxia,* characterized by unsteadiness and poor co-
ordination. Conditions which show spastic or athetoid movement features result from brain damage at birth usually caused
by oxygen starvation. As a result, the archetypal path of movement control is hindered and the child will continue to grow but
without the personality achieving a complete entry into its
bodily organism. There are degrees of movement disturbance
and it may only take a mild form in a hardly noticeable spastic
hand or foot position or an unusual slant to the position of the
head. At the other extreme there may be complete immobility
and hardly anything other than sensitive nursing care can be
offered.

Many of these children and youngsters have an intact intellectual capacity and it is obviously important that this is recognized. Great care is required in helping the individual to cope
with the discrepancy between inner experience and bodily dysfunction. A great deal has been achieved through providing

Pleasure and enhanced self-image in this person with cerebral palsy is encouraged by genuinely creative items of work.

special environments for the education of these children. In the case of the child who has also suffered severe intellectual impairment, attempts will have to be made to lead them towards controlled movement through which they can bring increased consciousness into their limbs.

Looking after such children provides the opportunity to watch them as they sleep. The usually stiff or uncontrolled limbs lie in the bed relaxed, the joints flexible. It is a moving experience to look into the eyes of the awakening child and as movement begins, the rigidity and other phenomena return. Such moments provide the conviction that in sleep the soul is elsewhere and waking life summons an active force into the body. The individual may appear to lead a life of continuous childhood, or even that of a baby, having to be fed, still wearing nappies and being taken for walks. They may also be regarded as small children as due to their lack of awareness they live in a state of emotional immaturity, sometimes miserable, sometimes laughing without any apparent cause. Like a toddler, they will reach out for a plate or tablecloth without any awareness of the consequences of such a spontaneous action.

Compassion, which does not mean pity, will surely arise in us when we allow our mind's eye to see, next to such a child, a freely moving, running, jumping schoolchild delighting in his own movement. If children with cerebral palsy are surrounded by loving devotion, and are offered therapeutic measures through music, speech, movement, massage and acceptance within ordinary social life, they will take in all of this and carry it with them into the future beyond the moment when they will leave behind this otherwise restricting bodily condition.

Always the unexpected: the hyperactive child
I first met James when he was seven years old — a small boy who was never still. He was always accompanied by an adult who would have to hold him by the hand. From his early years he had been hyperactive, always on the go, running or climbing. He would provoke and tease other children with his rapid, repetitive and jerky speech and at times he would go so far as to be physically and verbally aggressive, even dangerous. He threw stones and held long nails or knives out towards others, threatening and urging them to stop him. There was an obvious movement disturbance and he had a nervous tic in his face which caused him to grimace, and he was always talking. In class he would cause chaos by disrupting the lessons. Sleeping

was a problem and he had to have someone sitting outside his room in the evening to make sure he stayed in bed. He had other times when he would be just the opposite, showing warmth, being friendly and considerate.

I remember one occasion when we were walking along a street looking in shop windows. We went into a shop and suddenly he escaped my hand and dived under a rack of clothes. I leapt after him wondering what he was up to. Fortunately he had only found a piece of potato crisp which he had spotted out of the corner of his eye. You never knew what would happen next.

Although no comparison to James, the average two- or three-year-old with a lively mentality can be quite a handful. We all know parents who are in despair over their little one who has just spilt a bottle of ink over the carpet or nearly killed themselves pushing a knitting needle into the electricity socket.

The child described above suffers from an early childhood, post-encephalitic syndrome. Encephalitis describes an inflammatory condition resulting from fever which has caused damage to the brain. This may be caused by a childhood illness such as chicken-pox or measles or by vaccination or immunization. Whooping-cough vaccine is well known to the public as implicated in causing such damage to children. The child who suffers from brain damage due to encephalitis is the typically ill child who may suffer from a number of debilitating conditions which may leave them with multiple difficulties.

Such children are prone to disturbed patterns in sleep, they may rock, have great difficulty in understanding speech, have limited speech or none at all. They may have some autistic or psychotic features, laughing or acting on impulse seemingly prompted by, to us, unseen occurrences. Manual dexterity may be severely limited and affect feeding and the carrying out of other personal needs. They may be subject to convulsive disorders of a minor or serious nature and are often extremely difficult to care for and educate. In the home the parents will be driven to despair and residential special schooling is often the only possibility to aid the child educationally.

Injury to the brain and nervous system renders these children unable to attain adequate reflection and harmony within themselves. The hyperactive child will have to be helped to find inner order and peace.

Convulsive disorders
Carol is standing by the swing in a garden on a summer's afternoon. She is on holiday with her family and during the day they have been trying to make up their minds about what to do that evening. A certain amount of tension has built up because of differences of opinion, whether to go to the theatre or cinema or to go for a walk? Finally, it is decided to go and see a film. Carol has become increasingly irritable but settles down now that everything is resolved. All of a sudden her brother spots another film advertised in the newspaper and makes another suggestion: 'How about this one, this looks much better?' This is too much and whilst everybody else starts to talk again she reacts as if hit by lightning and falls to the ground in a convulsion.

She has suffered from epilepsy since being a small child. Everyone gathers round and helps. The afternoon plans are forgotten and the arguments accompanying the mood of the day are dramatically curtailed. Afterwards, when Carol has regained consciousness, she sleeps and is calm. It is obvious to everyone that the complexities of the day which were only the peak of what was anyway a rather tense holiday had affected them all but weighed most heavily on the one who had fallen to the ground. Once she had recovered the family went to the first film and spent an enjoyable evening together.

In another case, Richard is lying on the floor in an epileptic convulsion. His convulsions happen fairly regularly. He is someone who can hardly speak, can do very little and is occasionally extremely aggressive and hurts others. He lies there and someone is calling his name quietly to him. A bottle containing the herb rosemary is fetched and some of the lotion is applied to his forehead, temples and neck. The aroma has an invigorating and stimulating effect and it is as if, breath by breath, he regains consciousness and within a few minutes with eyes open and with movement returning to his face he is back on his feet. It is a remarkable example of how this plant oil can sometimes help in these situations.

Epilepsy is a convulsive disorder and is treated medically according to the degree of severity, *petit mal* or *grand mal*. If the condition is present in an otherwise normally developing child or adult then medical treatment will be the only obvious need. In the case of the child where convulsions are part of an overall complex of disabilities the epileptic condition will have to be considered as it manifests itself in the individual child. The *petit mal* condition showing as momentary absences will be regarded differently from the *grand mal* where there always exists a danger to life.

The two opening examples are not presented from a medical standpoint. In both cases the individuals were receiving medical support; in the first case convulsive episodes were rare but in the second, frequent and severe.

Involvement in such events leads to certain observations. Carol had experienced post-encephalitis trauma following immunization in early childhood. She possessed a tense personality and found it difficult to make contact with others. She was able in verbal and manual skills but with a demanding and almost hyperactive nature which if interfered with or arrested could lead to aggressiveness. Such children are often strong personalities, sensitive to their own inner experiences but with difficulties in being sensitive towards others. The build-up of tension, the attempt to cope with the inability to accept experiences and deal with them effectively, leads to a kind of dream-like relationship to the world.

In the first example there was a difficulty in coping with a given situation and this reached a climax in the convulsion. In retrospect Carol's convulsion was quite understandable and could possibly have been avoided. We can say that the organism into which the personality tries to enter is too heavy and dense and it cannot come successfully or sensitively through into the surrounding world. The effort to do so creates an inner tension, a struggle which is released in the convulsion after which the 'sky is clear' and the soul returns to a new found peace and tranquility. The child who is a partial dreamer tries to wake up but is thrown back, thrown out of his or her self and pulled dramatically down. The child is thrown across the threshold from waking to sleeping in an instant pathological process. This phenomenon is manifest in the shaking, the tension, the change of colour and so on.

The second episode of the waking up out of deep sleep, the drawing back of consciousness into the body after a period of unconsciousness, is a dramatic and almost magical example of what occurs after a convulsion. The soul life begins again as if breathed or pulled into the body and wakefulness. Instead of contributing to the circumstances which led to a convulsion, as in the first example, we should try to avoid such situations before it is too late. The child is out of balance with the world and finds itself hovering on the border between consciousness and unconsciousness. The challenge is to learn to read the individual characteristics of a child afflicted by such disorders of integration.

Over-sensitivity
In contrast to what has just been presented in the child who is wrestling to become integrated into its body and trying to gain a sensitive relationship to its surroundings, there is another child whose characteristic is over-sensitivity.

A boy approaches me in a deeply serious mood and tells me that he has been outside walking and as he passed a certain place he suddenly knew that his life had to change otherwise a great tragedy would descend on his family. Knowing that this child is not mentally deranged what can I make of such an experience? If I tell him to stop talking such nonsense, he will be mortally offended and from his point of view I will have failed to understand this profound inner experience as he 'knows it is true.' What is striking in this encounter is the look in the eyes, the earnest gaze looking into and through me. This boy gives the appearance of being too old, too serious for his age. His ideas and experiences get under other people's skin. To the unacquainted, such children can appear quite normal and interesting and initially attract a sympathetic response. Only in the course of time will the listener find out whether what they have heard is based on reality or not.

Ann is nice-looking, having delicate features but is immature, with poor speech, a little too attentive and aware of others. At times this gets out of hand and the attention and close awareness she has of others causes her great excitement and she begins to laugh and shake her head about, grabbing hold of you, and she has to be held back. Only gradually do you realize that the close awareness of yourself has led the child to change her habits and she has started to copy your mannerisms, for example, the way you eat and what you eat. She watches you over-attentively and gradually Ann's friendly nature begins to irritate. Inwardly you feel 'leave me alone' but to this she is insensitive. If you become openly annoyed and show you cannot stand up to this kind of close attention, you can become the focus of her lasting affection and preoccupation.

This child and others with similar tendencies are over-sensitive towards their surroundings and other people. They seem to have a sixth sense regarding how you are. If you are tired and not quite on top of life they can make your life a misery by taking advantage of this. This may seem an unkind thing to say but they are people who can easily be rejected and disliked by others who want to keep away from them. This very resistance by others to their sensitivity, gives rise to even more manifest behaviour problems and the child can become morose and morbid and extremes of attention-seeking behaviour can follow.

These children present a great challenge because they are looking for reassuring warmth but create the circumstances for rejection. Their behaviour can easily provoke anger because you want to push them back into themselves and out of your own personal space. It is necessary to help them to be more in themselves, to accept being in their own psychological space, but this is difficult for them to achieve.

Fragile X-syndrome
Only in the past decade has the so-called Fragile X-syndrome been described. The hereditary basis for this condition in the

child is not only revealed through genetic factors and abnormalities in the chromosome make-up but by similarities, in the
same way as with those affected by Down's syndrome. In the
case of Fragile X-syndrome, a fragile site, which may be an
abnormal gap towards the end of the chromosome, is present in
the female X-chromosome. Before the discovery of this syndrome these children were often confused with autistic children
as they also avoid eye-to-eye contact and do not answer direct
questions. They have similarities in gesture, in walking and in
speech. In 1968 Dr Lotte Sahlmann described the condition
before it became known as Fragile X-syndrome.[11] She referred
to it as a well defined syndrome having a 'total expression.' It
is important that these children are recognized as their shyness
is not due to autism but an extreme sensitivity towards others.

They have the capacity to sense the wellbeing of other
people. They are warm and helpful, constantly diverting attention from themselves by focussing their attention towards
others. One such child I know is always to be found a few
yards away by the hedge or door when I am having a private
conversation. When I look round, he will smile warmly and
look a bit embarrassed. I cannot be cross with him. He is
extremely polite, kind and helpful, asking continuously: 'How
are you? Nice day, nice day.' He knows the names of everyone
as well as how they are.

Aphasia
It is unusual to consider aphasia and dyslexia as sensory disturbances but these difficulties are related to the faculty of
hearing and two further developments beyond hearing, namely
the differentiation of sounds into language and meaning. This
can be regarded as the sensory landscape into which the child
has to find a way in the second and third years. The child who
babbles is surrounded by the spoken word but does not speak
until miraculously the sounding of the word evokes a resonance
in them through a form of refined imitation. This is both a
receptive and an executive process. In some children, who are
clearly not deaf, sounds are heard but words do not emerge or
become distinct and because of this they cannot understand

speech. This condition is known as receptive aphasia. There are other children who can understand language and respond to verbal instruction, but they cannot speak to you in a coherent way. This is known as executive aphasia.

Aphasia has sometimes been mistaken for autism when serious withdrawal and forms of contact disturbance are observed. However, aphasic children are not autistic even if they are bereft of the basic elements of verbal communication. Autism can be a secondary condition as a result of the contact disturbance. If we recall earlier comments regarding child development, it is obvious that the aphasic child has been unable to achieve what should have appeared as a second major milestone, namely speech. The growing down and taking hold of the body in progressive steps which lead to walking, speaking and thinking are the main achievements in early childhood. Aphasia results from the failure of this movement refinement and the individual is unable to walk, as it were, into the landscape of language and meaning. Therefore, it is understandable

Individual attention helps this aphasic child who finds it difficult to link images to the spoken and written word.

Drama therapy stimulates responsiveness, phantasy and participation in this aphasic child.

that in addition to the use of various sound- and language-based methods, an important direction for therapy is to be found in movement exercises, especially the controlled movements which are present in eurythmy and curative eurythmy (see p.74). Both of these affect the subtle movement organization in the child.

It is important that aphasia is correctly diagnosed as profound difficulties are encountered by individuals who live in a world of communicating people without being able to communicate themselves. It is like living continuously in a foreign country which has an incomprehensible language. For the speaking person this experience is probably mild compared to the experience of the aphasic child. Lack of appreciation of the communication difficulties of the aphasic child can lead to intense frustration in them and may lead to aggressive, disturbed behaviour.

Dyslexia

In the early part of this chapter reading and writing were described as ways in which communication develops beyond basic language into means of expression where thoughts and ideas can be shared. Through the acquisition of these faculties the field of language is extended beyond hearing, word differentiation and meaning, into the social arena of communication and we become citizens of the world. We probably all have an adult friend who has a dyslexic tendency and avoids self-expression in reading or writing. Writing is a particular problem even though these days dyslexia has become better understood and is no longer regarded as a social stigma.

The imaginative experience of the child between the time of the acquisition of speech up to the beginning of reading and writing calls for a change from imaginative experience, picture forming, into the seemingly abstract world of letters. Therefore, the way and the age at which children are faced with having to learn to read and write is of great significance. Sensitivity to potential difficulties such as dyslexia requires special attentiveness. A help for the child with regard to dyslexia and related learning difficulties is the imaginative approach found in the curriculum of the early classes of the Waldorf or Rudolf Steiner Schools. This curriculum recognizes the imaginative quality of the child's inner experience and only gradually leads them to what we know as reading and writing.

Widening the spectrum

If our concepts of normality and abnormality in child development are widened we can begin to speak of the average development of the child. We no longer describe the normal or abnormal child but only 'children.' In today's terms this is an 'holistic' approach, a landscape within which there is a varied spectrum of all possible colours.

Parents, teachers and others who meet lots of children notice the kind of tendencies which have already been mentioned: the child who is always sunny and lovable, the withdrawn child, the insensitive and the over-sensitive child. These subtle tendencies are not difficult to perceive as general traits in different children. It is only if the trait develops into something about which the parent or teacher becomes particularly conscious, then the characteristic will attain special interest. A further aspect in this anthropology of childhood is that of the large-headed or hydrocephalic child and the small-headed or microcephalic child.

The large-headed child

I remember taking part in a case conference. The man who chaired the meeting had never met the boy in question before and allowed him to talk freely and express his thoughts. The boy presented a wonderful picture of himself as quiet, considerate, helpful and devoted to the needs of others. He also spoke about a number of interests which he had not been helped to develop by the school. He said he was not given enough time

This large-headed child is already 'out there,' even as the teacher tries to create a rhythmic co-ordination exercise.

to be by himself. In that setting it was difficult to add the other
side to what he had said because he sounded so plausible. In his
charming way of speaking, the rather grand presentation, the
gentle and thoughtful choice of words, he was perfectly understandable except to those who knew him and lived with him. In
reality he was a rather noisy person and far from his not having
enough time for peace and quiet, the people who lived with him
would have loved him to spend more time on his own because
he was unable to leave others alone. The interests he wanted to
pursue were quite unrealistic and the ones he spoke about and
professed a wish to develop were ones he had never even mentioned before. As for helping others, his attempts often caused
more trouble than they were worth. This example may well
seem trivial. What does it matter if such a child embellishes the
truth? You can let such a child say what he wishes but if you
want to help him you may begin to recognize certain characteristics in the personality.

There are children whom we know as hydrocephalic and
who are subject to what we call chronic large-headedness. At
birth these children have a head which weighs as much as the
rest of the body. A stage through which everyone passes in
embryological development and which we can call 'large-
headedness' is retained through the pregnancy and carried into
early childhood. This 'large-headedness' becomes a determining
factor in a child's life and it has been noticed that even if
medical intervention has been able to alleviate the head water
and reduce the head size, there are tendencies which remain.

Like the child in embryo, the upper head of these children
predominates over the face which in itself is round and full.
The child is typically late in sitting, standing and walking, the
fontanelle remains open longer than usual and often the child
has a noticeably strong connection to the mother. Imagination
will dominate over the intellect and an active imagination and
artistic inclination will lead the child towards fantasy rather
than reason. Concentration in school will be difficult and subjects like mathematics will pose particular problems. There is
usually a phlegmatic temperament and there will be little appli-
cation to practical work.

Speech may have appeared early in childhood and a certain articulate quality will lead to the appearance of superiority. Because of this these children can veer from being excessively gentle and almost royal to being irritable, impatient and aggressive if they are contradicted or challenged.

The small-headed child
If the large-headed child is like a prince riding in a stately carriage along a tree-lined avenue with a driver, coachmen and servants in attendance, the small-headed child is like a racing-car driver tearing round the track. Instead of demure attendants these children will be the motor mechanics with head and hands at work on the engine, covered in oil and grime.

In extreme cases there will be those with pathologically small heads pinched at the temples who find it extremely difficult to progress educationally. They will be small, probably of pale complexion with a pointed face, receding forehead, a closed fontanelle at birth, and long-limbed. Having large hands they will be skilful and tend to be mechanical and over-interested in details. Unlke the large-headed child, they are wide awake, easily distracted, untidy and too busy rushing around to look after their possessions. They are always on the go and in school they will probably be information gatherers. It will be difficult to lead them towards imaginative learning and abstract ideas as these require fantasy.

In a school play it was interesting to have to direct two of the players, one of whom shared the first tendency of being a dreamer and the other who was small, wiry and wide awake. Whatever I did I could not bring the small-headed boy to act as if he were a royal personality. Despite all the costuming and fine frills he remained looking like a workman. The clothes did not look right and he had no style. He also wanted to direct everyone and kept on telling them what to do and was quite upset at the stupid people who did not do what he said. It was a kind of Pygmalion effort to transform the pauper into a prince. The large-headed dreamer, on the other hand, could hardly be brought into the play as he could not involve himself in the flow of the action. He had a natural presence on stage and would not have needed to have spoken a word to put over a sense of being a significant personality. However, as far as drama was concerned he was completely ineffective.

In appearance the large-headed child seems to retain characteristics of early childhood, as shown by the roundness of the head, the gentleness and softness of hands and limbs. The small-headed, over-awake child is angular and thin. The one goes through the world aloof with head held up and back, the other walks or rushes with head forward. The more one contemplates these characteristics, the more one is moved by the mystery of the human form and its potential in expressing and reflecting different human characteristics. The conditions required by the soul are developed in a time of unconsciousness, in the embryo and in early childhood. As time goes by, they begin to show themselves and become recognizable as the individual's physical and personality traits. This phenomenon is particularly apparent in the example of the contrast between the large-headed and the small-headed child, physiologically and psychologically.

Colours in the spectrum

The walker on the hills on a late winter's afternoon stops in his tracks to view the setting sun and its afterglow of colours. The sunrise had been pale yellow, pink and green and above a deep blue. Now the clouds and sky are vibrant red and orange, the soft hillsides violet and indigo. The rainbow he saw at midday seemed to him like a fine condensation of all the colours that played about him at dawn and now at dusk, filling the heavens and defining the moors and fields.

The children described in this chapter are characterizations, colours of childhood. We may try to find the norm or average but when we look more closely, and try to see 'things as they are,' we discover a spectrum of colours within childhood which is as varied as there are individuals but in which we also find similarities, blues and greens. At first children are light, only later becoming heavier and bearing the needs of the world on their own shoulders, for better or worse. Some may make their way in life with utmost seriousness, others in a light-hearted manner; some as realists, others as dreamers, artists.

We may conclude that the children we have encountered in this chapter are more visible, stand out in the landscape with greater definition and in their especially vibrant or deep colouring are somehow different and extraordinary. Because of this they do not readily merge in the landscape of our expectations of normal child development. We do not want to eradicate their special qualities but to try and help them to make their journey and way through life with fulfilment.

The life of any child leads away from the arms of the mother and reaches out towards the other goal at death. In between is life and its destiny. The child is not alone on this journey and it matters how its destiny develops and that its colour and finer hues are recognized. Curative education finds its purpose in perceiving the colours of the child and attempting to lead the child from what is often its limited place in the spectrum into movement within a wider sea of colours.

4. The curative educational environment

To present childhood as a spectrum in which differences are compared to colours in the rainbow may well seem naive. However, contemplation of this imagination can help us to consider the child with special needs as having its place alongside other children but standing out from the average and lending an interesting and different quality of colour to the landscape of childhood.

An important starting point in curative education is to regard differences in individuals as justified and necessary. Wanting to discover the meaning and value in every child and every youngster is a primary attribute. Ideas of human equality and the use of non-judgmental terminology stem from a wish to recognize the inherent spirituality and integrity of the child. This is right and is an achievement of human thinking and perception. We are able to meet the child with special needs as an individual having its own meaning within the overall image of childhood. All children are engaged in integrating their evolving self into their constitutional bodily reality and into their social and cultural context. Therefore, the historical perspective presented earlier is important. The child with a particular problem will be helped or hindered in its development depending on whether in one century it is regarded as an idiot or imbecile or, in another, as a child like any other child but having certain specific learning difficulties or special needs.

Attitudes

> *You have no idea how unimportant it is what the*
> *teacher says or does in comparison to the*
> *importance of who he is as a person, as a teacher.*
>   Rudolf Steiner

The primary attitude in curative education is one of compassion, leading to the will to help. Compassion in this sense is not a Franciscan quality or pity. It is more like empathy, requiring active involvement. As R.D. Laing put it: 'the attempt to experience the experience of the other person.'

Involvement in the life of such children as have been described leads those who are their parents or teachers to discover limitations in their understanding and perception of the child's needs. The question arises as to whether you can in fact understand the needs of a particular child? You may have to face doubt and uncertainty. Have you the courage to try to help, to risk a particular approach? Curative education demands this kind of interest and involvement. You will not be able to help unless you are willing to step into the uncertain territory of not knowing whether you can help. This dilemma is particularly apparent at the outset of work in curative education but will always be present as you can never be certain of any particular approach. Through experience, training and research you will always be able to modify and develop your therapeutic work.

The parents

Parents of children such as those described in Chapter 3 are understandably bound in a deep subjective involvement with their children. All kinds of thoughts may pass through their minds: What went wrong? Are we to blame? Maybe it would have been better if she had not survived? What will happen after we have gone? If we had done things differently she may not have been like this? Look at the strain this is placing on our other children! These kinds of burdened reactions are not experienced by all such parents. Many have found meaning and have understood the significance of having a child with special qualities.

We can ask whether curative education can be effective in the parental home? It should be possible for curative education to help in all situations and one of these may be the parental home, supported by a day school. However, we have to realize that because of the close involvement which parents build up with their child it often helps to give the child an opportunity to be within a fully curative educational environment, at least for a time.

Being at home

In some instances it may be impossible to help a child if it remains in the family home. In such cases a period spent in a residential curative school may be the answer. In non-residential schools teachers are not involved in the home life or leisure time of their pupils. Their main concern is with the active, waking life of their pupils. However involvement in the home life makes it possible for the teacher to extend his or her attention to the night or sleep life of the child.

The relationship of day-time to night-time, of our waking life to our sleeping life, forms one of the greatest archetypes in human experience. We know that satisfaction coming from an active, purposeful life is the best kind of preparation for a refreshing night's sleep. Disturbed sleep patterns lead to irritability, dissatisfaction and other adverse symptoms.

A few years ago a neighbour and friend of a curative school stopped one of the teachers and said they had noticed that a number of the children in the school had recently begun to 'walk differently,' appeared to be more purposeful in their way of walking compared to when he had first seen them. Now this school had gone through a difficult time and had only recently been reorganized and restructured. The teachers had realized

Laying the table.

that an ordered, warm, enthusiastic environment was essential
for their pupils' progress. A well cared-for environment had
been created, with nutritious food, attractive surroundings, with
a lively educational, social and leisure programme. The curriculum timetable had been newly devised and the school was generally in good shape with the teachers working well together.

It may seem strange to equate this kind of order and wellbeing with the way some pupils had been seen to be walking.
Of course this is an image, a way of looking at things, of equat-
ing activity to results. The difficulty in accepting that education
which is carried out over the day has a real effect even into the
way a child walks is due, in part, to a lack of appreciation for

Celebrating a birthday.

the significance of our nights, our sleep. It is in the sleeping life that the benefits of education and therapy and so on are integrated into our ongoing life, even into our movement development. It is crucial that curative education recognizes this fact. The teacher, therapist and educator will find a source of moral strength in realizing not only the importance of what they do, what they teach, but also of how they go about their work, whether with enthusiasm or otherwise. The night will always judge the value or poverty of the day and in this case the value of the educator's work. The children will show their teacher, verbally or otherwise, whether the teaching is bearing good fruit or is encouraging apathy, restlessness and so on.

Therefore the home life, alongside school time, should set out to create a healthy, ordered and wholesome setting, helping the child to feel *at home*.

Some children clearly do not seem to feel at home, even in their family house. They may not even have a concept of home. Some are hardly at home in their bodies. Others are strangers to ordinary relationships or at loggerheads with the world, maybe aggressively so. To help a group of children with such diverse needs to be able to share a home together, to eat at the same table, to wash-up, sweep the floor and do the household jobs, to stand still for a few minutes to sing a seasonal song or say a verse or poem around a lighted candle can be a considerable challenge.

The educator

The descriptions made in the previous chapter arise from observations of children made over a period of time. Working in the field of curative education for a number of years, enables one to recognise most of the descriptions of children in the previous chapter as either overt or subtle characteristics. Interest in the subtleties showing in the child, their personality and difficulties, be they cognitive, sensory, verbal, emotional or motor, develops the observation-based experience of the educator. 'Educator' is used here in the broad sense for those who apply themselves in assisting a child's development and is not restricted to the classroom or school situation. An educator is someone who is aiding the child in a considered and purposeful manner.

Both observation and experience help to develop the means by which you can characterize the child's needs. Building-up such a picture will take into account the personality of the child, their difficulties and destiny, their family context and other circumstances. These steps eventually open the way to a tentative diagnosis. Diagnosis is used here in a broad sense. What is observed and experienced can be understood and formed into something of value as a therapeutic insight.

This kind of diagnostic endeavour is meant to assist the

curative educator's therapeutic response to the child. It is not a matter of finding a 'solution to the problem' but a starting point for a response. The educator always lives with questions such as these: How shall I respond to this child? Am I the best one to help? In this field of work these are necessary questions as it may be that you are not the right person and someone else will be much more effective. Selflessness, an overcoming of vanity and the development of objectivity with regard to the child's needs and your own therapeutic ability are vital. When therapeutic intervention is being considered, a collegial group way of working is essential. In such a setting the doctor, teacher, therapist and educator can share observations and develop a helpful diagnostic picture of the child's needs and from this therapeutic work can begin.

Sharing a meal.

The environment

A collegial way of working is essential to curative education as
the needs of the children we are considering cannot be met by
the doctor, teacher or therapist alone. Only by working together
can each one add a different possibility to the overall therapeutic attempt. Because of this, curative education in the home,
as practised by the parent, will always present limitations and
it may well prove to be impossible to develop the kind of
objectivity which is needed.

Schooling is a natural phase in the child's life and for those
with particular needs the usual school setting will only be helpful if specialized teaching outside the general curriculum is
available. If the necessary awareness and experience is present
then a curative educational environment may be able to be
created within the framework of the home together with the day
school, whether this be the usual school with a remedial class
or a specialized school. A number of the children who were
described earlier suffered from a complex of difficulties and a
curative educational environment created for their needs proved
to be the best setting for them to spend part of their childhood.
The period of childhood is a formative time and the right therapeutic help at this stage can be of inestimable value for later
life.

The curriculum

Education, in the usual sense, involves the imparting of knowledge and the bringing forth of the inherent capacities of the
child. Curative education calls for a multi-disciplinary, therapeutic situation directed to specific needs. It usually has to do
with those children who, in the first place, have significant
difficulties in acquiring knowledge and show limited interest or
ability to learn.

Although anthroposophical curative education is multi-
disciplinary it has a focus in the classroom, particularly in the

A form drawing exercise aids spatial orientation and fine motor co-ordination, preparing the way for writing.

case of younger children. Pre-school work can be attempted but the main emphasis will be on introducing the child to the Waldorf curriculum. This curriculum is used throughout the Waldorf and Steiner Schools, whether these are for the normally developing child or for the child with special needs. It is based on the view that the early development of a child reflects te cultural development of humanity and civilisation as a whole.

This means that the younger child of about six or seven years of age will find that the motifs of the fairy-tale are in harmony with its inner experiences. The child at that age lives in an imaginative world and finds a natural affinity with the world of the princes and princesses, the king and queen, the woodcutter and the fishes and birds whose language can be understood. Living in this world, the child will be led into play, building castles, dressing-up and re-creating these events pic-torially.

After fairy-tales comes the time of fables. These stories are often about animals and the child already begins to turn away from the world of images which were found in something like the Grimm fairy tales. Fables and stories lead into mythology; the Old Testament, followed by the Norse, Persian, Egyptian, Greek and Roman mythology. At each stage the enactment of scenes from these mythologies and poetic presentations will be experienced by the child.

In the Waldorf curriculum the main themes of human devel-opment, characterized by fairy-tales leading to mythologies, connect the child's inner experiences to the evolution of human-ity and with this the child takes part in a process of personal integration into the world. This curriculum presents a common heritage, though this will be modified where it is used in dif-ferent parts of the world. History will only be introduced in the pre-puberty and puberty time and the progress of civilization into European history leading to the Renaissance and up to modern times will then be discovered. Emphasis is focused on these later periods in the so-called upper school curriculum which covers the final years of secondary education.

This basic outline describes the curriculum starting in the

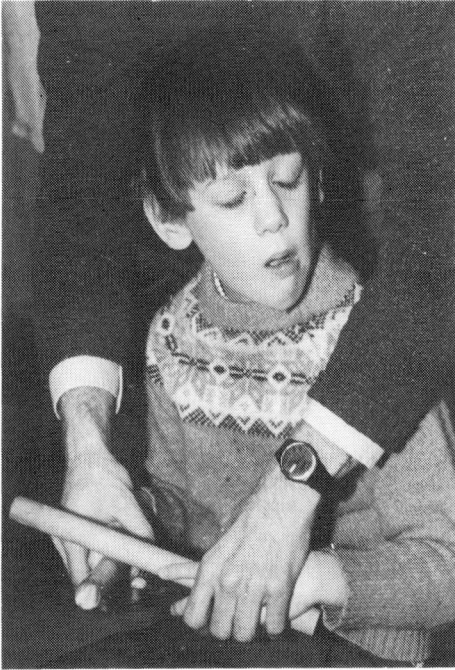

A simple exercise to wake up.

lower classes with a predominantly imaginative approach and leading progressively towards the modern consciousness with science, technology and the study of the twentieth century. Alongside and interwoven with the main lesson subjects which present general cultural development will be related subjects; geography, languages, literature, mathematics and so on. Teaching in the lower classes emphasises an artistic approach through poetry, painting, drawing, music and play. Dramatic recreations will be used whenever possible. Even in the introduction to writing and reading an artistic approach will be used in order to hold back the development of the intellect in the early years as at this stage the small child is predominantly imaginative in outlook. Overstimulation of the intellect in the early years can be seen as inappropriate and potentially harmful.

Rudolf Steiner regarded the Waldorf curriculum as a medicine for children growing up in the twentieth century. It can help the child to develop inner faculties through its own capacities instead of being fenced in with set curriculum demands against which he or she is measured, marked and graded.

In the context of the Waldorf curriculum children with learning difficulties will reveal a variety of problems in engaging with and assimilating subject-matter. This should not lead to the less able children being held back in the lower classes. The same possibility should hold good for the child with learning difficulties as for any other, meaning that at each age a particular subject-matter should be encountered. In schools for children with learning difficulties which make use of the Waldorf curriculum the child will progress through the school according to their chronological age and not according to individual ability. This is seen to do justice to the inherent developmental phase of the child.

The teacher

The teacher's task is to take the subject-matter and find ways of bringing this to the children irrespective of their individual abilities. This presents a considerable challenge as in a typical class there may be children who are withdrawn or unmotivated, those who appear to live in a dream, who are hyperactive or have specific motor difficulties. They may have sensory disturbances or be unable to speak. The teachers will have to exercise all their imaginative powers and creativity as their aim should be to give each child a sense of being part of a class.

Learning

The children should not sense that they are handicapped but that they have work to do if they are to learn. Education, often being regarded as a mainly intellectual pursuit with its goal in academic attainment, requires a different approach in the case of children with learning difficulties. Learning is usually taken to be dependent on memory and intelligence. With children who find it difficult to learn we discover that what we call the *will* plays a significant and vital part in the process of learning. Our description of children in Chapter 3 was not made on the basis of intellectual capacities but rather on differences in 'engagement.'

Of course, we shall encounter difficulties in writing and reading, memory, comprehension and so on, but if a child is withdrawn or dreamy, hyperactive or suffers from fixations you will not be able to catch their interest or engage them in learning unless something else is done. It is a discovery of curative education that it is the *will* that has to be addressed in the child who has a learning difficulty. Observation of different children tells us that disturbances of the will are also revealed by characteristic movement disturbances.

Taking a basic contrast between, for example, a hyperactive child and a withdrawn child, the teacher has the same aim in mind, to help them to learn, but will have to approach each one in a different way. The hyperactive child will have to be drawn into itself, to withdraw from preoccupation with its surroundings, be brought to rest. The withdrawn child will have to be encouraged to take an interest in the world, to become involved.

The curative teacher usually approaches the class with the above in mind. Lessons will begin in a consistent manner, perhaps with a poem or song appropriate to the time of the year. Through a variety of rhythmic exercises using the hands and feet, or rhythmic walking and other movements, even using sticks or bean-bags for throwing, for instance, the children are engaged, become attentive and are encouraged to listen. The main lesson subject is then presented according to the curriculum age of the class. Following this presentation the class will then undertake personal work on the subject content.

The teacher will have to use all his or her creativity to bring about an encounter between the will of the child, in as far as it has been activated and harmonized, and the subject-matter itself. In this process it is the class which is the focus. The aim is to enable a differentiated group of children to become a class

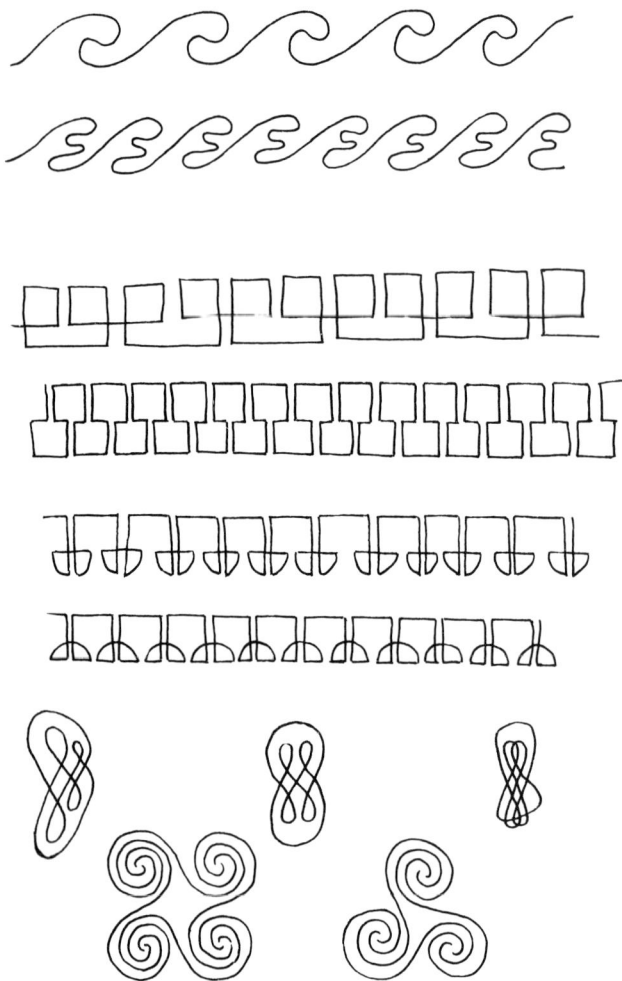

Form drawing in the classroom.

and have an experience which is beyond and other than the experience of each individual. This is an important way of addressing the spiritual integrity of a child aside from their particular difficulties. Education which is imaginative and which strengthens the will helps the child with learning difficulties to acquire the means to learn and the inner peace needed in order to listen.

After the main subject lesson will come a second lesson and usually additional teaching help will be called on. The children will work at writing, reading and numeracy in ways appropriate to their abilities. This work is not simply a matter of pencil and paper and the use of word processors but should address disturbances of will and disturbance of motor co-ordination. Because of this, writing takes a priority over reading and every means will be used to lead the child into basic writing skills. This may be helped by walking the forms of letters on the floor, by drawing them in creative ways on the blackboard, by painting and by dynamic drawing exercises. In curative education repeated practice of these exercises is used to help correct imbalances.

It is not possible to go into greater detail as for each child the approach will be different and this is so because the Waldorf curriculum and curative teaching are not methods but approaches requiring the creative involvement of the teacher if they are to be of any value.

Creativity and an artistic approach underlie all curative educational work. An imaginative approach will have to be found to address the needs of each child. This can only be attempted if the teacher makes the effort to train his or her observation and to develop flexibility in teaching. The teacher has to be permeated by the qualities of enthusiasm and love for the child. It is also necessary that the teacher develops determination and commitment towards the child. There must be the conviction that the child will be able to learn and to reach beyond its limitations even if these limitations are at times a source of frustration both for the child as well as for the teacher.

A further help in engaging the child is through movement,

Project work in the older classes.

and eurythmy in particular (see p.77). Eurythmy is an art of movement developed by Rudolf Steiner and is particularly helpful as it is a creative medium which can respond to individual needs and enhances the experience of self in relation to space and balance. Body images can be discovered physically but also through movement and gesture, in space and in relation to tone. Curative eurythmy which is used to help specific movement disorders will be described later in this chapter.

Bothmer gymnastics, developed from indications given by Rudolf Steiner, helps to develop spatial awareness and coordination by using harmonious rhythmic exercises and therapeutic games.

Handwork is an important subject; knitting, sewing and other

Becoming still before letting go.

handwork activities in the Lower Classes; woodwork, pottery, needlework and other craft work in the Upper Classes. All of these help to refine motor co-ordination.

The upper school

As the child develops, it gradually encounters the capacity for intellectual thinking which begins to predominate in the pre-puberty and adolescent phases. Science and technology are studied as examples of applied thinking; experiments and other investigations are meant to lead the child into forming conclusions. Youngsters have to think, and to do this they have to acquire accurate observation.

The adolescent years are not easy for any youngster but especially not for those who labour under certain difficulties which limit their intellectual and emotional growth. After some years of experience with the Waldorf curriculum in a curative educational setting, it can be hoped that the feeling life of the child will have become harmonized and that they will have developed an interest in the world. These are the inner challenges of the adolescent years: to find inner harmony and to develop interests. If this can be achieved by the adolescent with learning difficulties, they will have gained something valuable which can support them on their path towards adulthood.

'Well, how does it work?'

Therapies

In the classroom the child develops within a social context. This context is formed by the experience of being in a group, working and learning together and by relating to the world through the class subjects. At the same time the work entailed in mastering the complexities of writing and reading, number work and so on, create the tools through which the child becomes a communicator and can also receive what the world has to offer by way of knowledge and information.

The teacher will encounter the child as an individual, particularly through the difficulties the child has in progressing with class work as in writing and reading for example. However, the children we are discussing will have needs which cannot be met solely in the context of the classroom. The teacher may well be the one who will say this child cannot progress further in the classroom unless he receives specific individual help. It is at this point that a particular therapeutic activity may be indicated.

A therapeutic situation implies a considered intervention into the child's life. Such intervention is necessary because the tendencies and difficulties of the child are perceived as restrictive to their development.

In curative education therapeutic work is carried out under the supervision of a doctor. The doctor and the therapist take the same kind of responsibility. A therapy will be prescribed in a similar way to a medicine and only those who are fully trained in their particular therapeutic discipline can take this kind of responsibility.

Curative eurythmy

The aim of a therapy is to harmonize and bring into balance tendencies which limit the child's integration into the body and hinder meaningful interaction with their surroundings. Under 'Learning' (see p.70) it was described how the curative teacher tries to bring the class into a condition of readiness to learn. If the pupils are running about, shouting, laughing or are withdrawn, movement exercises will be a help in drawing together

Attaining balance: step by step.

the diverse tendencies within the class group. Eurythmy is an artistic and social movement activity which can further help the child towards a finer sense for its particular position in space.

Curative eurythmy has been developed as a therapeutic measure in which the therapist in consultation with a doctor takes a child's tendency or complex of tendencies and creates an interactive sequence of movement exercises which are specific to the individual child. These may take the form of specially developed movements and gestures or an exercise with a ball, a rod or a stick or whatever means the therapist finds to focus on the particular tendency. Curative eurythmy works on the sensory experience of the child: touch, spatial orientation, the sense of life in its liveliness or apathy, its expression and movement, also the relationship to space from below to above, back to front and left to right.

In Chapter 3 it was pointed out how movement can be regarded as the primary motivating force in child development, giving rise not only to actual manual dexterity, uprightness and walking but also to speech and articulation. It can also be regarded as the subtle presence in organic function and dysfunction. Curative eurythmy attempts to connect the movements inherent in speech which have been discovered as related to the formative movements in the organic system, to specific disturbances in the individual child. Through this, archetypal harmonizing movements are brought to bear on a particular condition and tendency.

Art therapy
Art therapy as found in curative education is not based on the psycho-analytical diagnostic model. Instead, the attempt is made to find a starting point for understanding the child and the task of the therapist is to use an artistic medium to lead the child through a healing and harmonizing process. In other words, one does not let a child express itself in a so-called free way *ad infinitum*. With children with special needs as well as with

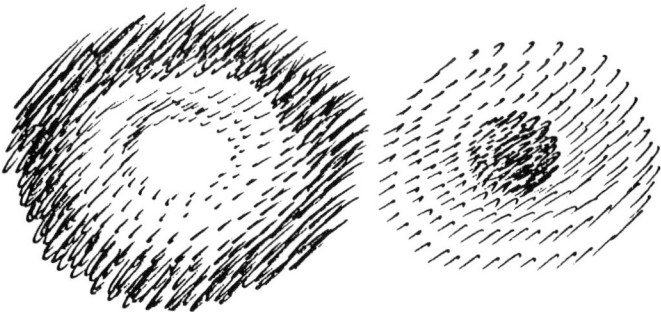

Two basic forms: opening up and closing in.

*Large scale assisted painting exercises lead children with movement
and engagement disturbances to greater control,
often with beautiful results.*

anyone else we are rarely free to express what lives in ourselves and most of the time what lives in us as our inner experience is far from free, being subject to all kinds of limitations and unconscious tendencies.

A child who is tense and cramped will express itself in one way and a hysteric or hyper-sensitive child in another. The aim is to develop a healing process which can gradually work on the specific difficulties of the child in the same way as a medicine might be prescribed and administered over a period of time. Usually, the following questions will be asked: 'In the case of this child, is painting the best medium or would modelling or black and white drawing be better?' 'If painting is the right medium, shall I emphasise blue or red, yellow or green?' 'Does the child require strong forms and images or only a colour experience?' In art therapy what is within the child, its inner experience, begins to reveal itself and the therapist has to be careful in exposing the child to its own tendencies.

Music therapy
Music in its different forms can have a powerful influence on the human being. Today, music in its modern manifestations is used to create mood, to relax by, as a background and so on. In its more refined nature it can evoke a profound emotional or even spiritual response. Witness how a Bach cantata, a Beethoven symphony or a Bartok quartet can address the individual in a way which reaches into the invisible, indestructible parts of the soul. The organs of hearing and listening as with the other middle senses or 'apparent senses,' smell, taste and so on, form the bridges from the experience of the self within to the world beyond self.

The basic elements of music are melody, harmony and beat and, when understood, the use of tones, intervals and rhythm can be used to evoke a therapeutic effect. The sound arising in the surrounding of the child is heard and, in the way implied above, depending on the intentions of the therapist, will resound and work on within the child. It is obvious, when we consider the effect of music, that it is not a matter only of hearing music. Music resonates within the human being and we

'Did you hear the tone?'

know that beat can be used to create excitement; rhythm is
present physiologically in the breathing and circulation and in
various structures of the body.

Based on the therapist's and doctor's image of the child
whether it has an epileptic quality, is pre-psychotic and so on
the therapy will be developed from musical elements. The evolving therapy may lead to a receptive listening experience for
the child or an active participation using a range of suitable
instruments. It may also call for movement. Music therapy aims
to strengthen auditory orientation of the child which is the other
side to visual orientation.

Today, children, as well as we ourselves, are strongly orien-
tated to the visual world. Music and sound reach inwards and,
for example, where the psychotic child has become trapped in

a visual perception, music can be used to free or loosen the child from within. In seeing we gain a visual orientation to the outer world. In listening or hearing, in speech and music, meaning is addressed. In a subtle, artistic and non-intellectual way, the disturbed child can be brought to an inner experience of rest and security. Music can be healing for certain children who live their lives in a seemingly chaotic and meaningless inner condition. In this sense music therapy can bring nourishment and harmony to the inner life.

Coloured light therapy
A therapy which is still in its early stages of development is coloured light therapy. It unites elements of the above mentioned mediums of eurythmy, colour and music. Coloured light

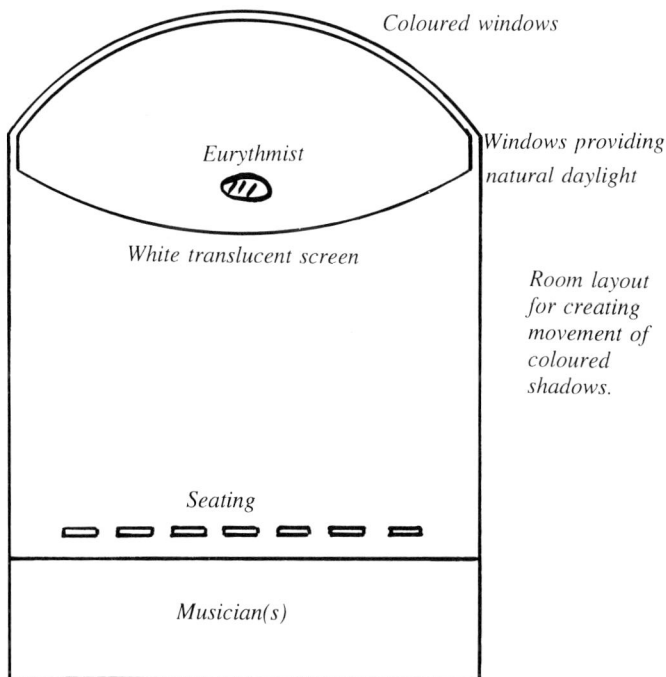

Coloured windows

Eurythmist

Windows providing natural daylight

White translucent screen

Room layout for creating movement of coloured shadows.

Seating

Musician(s)

therapy aims to help in harmonizing and ordering the process of breathing. Breathing, in this sense, is meant not only as a physiological process but describes the rhythmic relating of inner experience to outer perceptions, between the activity of the head, the thinking dimension of the human being and the more unconscious dimension of the limbs and the will.

Curative education will often be concerned with those whose breathing is out of balance, with children who are unable to find inner peace. Certain archetypal tendencies were touched on in Chapter 3 and many of the children described can be helped to attain a harmonization of inner experience through coloured light therapy.

A quiet room is chosen and lit only by different coloured windows each of which can either be blanked out or allowed to let in natural light. Colours fall onto a stretched, translucent white screen and in front of the screen a eurythmist makes slow, considered movements. The effect of each colour streaming from behind the eurythmist is to create coloured shadow forms on the screen. The child sits in the room on the other side of the screen and witnesses the flowing beauty of the play of forms and colours. While this is happening music is played from behind.

Although this therapy is largely unknown it is being researched in a few schools. It has already been discovered that children can be brought into an enhanced condition of harmony through the healing effect of the working together of these artistic media.

Other therapies
In this context we have only mentioned four specific therapies; curative eurythmy, art therapy, music therapy and coloured light therapy. It would also be justified to continue in describing other therapeutic methods such as speech therapy, play therapy, drama therapy, horse-riding therapy, individual counselling and psychotherapy, as well as the more direct therapies, for example, rhythmical massage, oil dispersion bath treatment and so on.

However, our aim is only to indicate that alongside and

working together with what we know as the classroom and educational aspect of curative education are a number of specific therapeutic disciplines. Education and therapy form two of the main approaches within curative education, working hand in hand and focusing on the needs of the child.

Medical aspects

One of the most interesting questions we can ask when considering children with so called special needs is, whether or not they are ill? Is what we used to call mental handicap an illness? A simple answer is that such conditions as we have described are not illnesses even if they originated in a time of illness, an encephalitic trauma in early childhood, for example. We could rather say that whatever has led to the child's condition, as far as we can discover this, has also led to the child becoming different. The child has been thrust into a new condition of experience, a kind of post-illness condition which may not manifest in what we would call illness but rather as a condition of experience. What part do the doctor and medical treatment play in curative education?

Hopefully it is becoming clear that the approach taken by anthroposophical curative education is based on the view that the child we are concerned with is taking part in a progressive, ever changing and developing relationship between an inner quality, call it a spiritual or soul dimension, and its manifest, physical characteristics. Our consciousness emerges as our inner spiritual dimension integrates into and forms our physical organism. In this sense our bodily organism is a manifestation of our self and gives us the basis for identity and self-image.

The task of the doctor whose orientation is found through anthroposophy is to attempt to understand the relationship of the soul to the bodily condition and to what could be called the integration of the self into these. The treatment prescribed will aim to help the healthy integration of the different facets of the child. For example, to help the breathing process in a child where there is anxiety or fixation. This kind of treatment

requires considerable insight and this presents a challenge to
medical practice. It is not a matter of alleviating symptoms in
the child but of strengthening and fostering healing forces within the organism. The means of treatment, where it involves
medication, will make use of homeopathic medicaments prescribed out of an anthroposophical point of view.

The collegial meeting

At the beginning of the first chapter we encountered Peter and
it was said that he would undoubtedly have benefited from curative education in his early years. By now it is probably obvious
that curative education is not about offering set answers to one
or another difficulty encountered in a particular child. Rather,
it is an attempt to create, as one observer put it, a 'nurturing
environment as therapy.' The timbers and bricks of the therapeutic environment are the teachers with their experience and
knowledge gained through their working lives.

The same holds good for the children mentioned in Chapter 3. Each one is described from a particular standpoint, of
epilepsy or of large-headedness and so on. There is no magic
answer to such conditions. They have to be recognized and
understood and the attempt made to find out what helps. Individuals cannot be narrowed down to a simple characterization. It
is the whole child who must be understood.

The collegial meeting draws together all aspects of curative
educational work. In the setting of a well-prepared meeting, all
participants — doctors, therapists, teachers, house parents and
others — attempt to place their combined experience and observations at the disposal of the meeting which is to concern itself
with a particular child. The collegial meeting has four parts.
Firstly, the physical characteristics of the child and its development to date are given. Secondly, an outline of the immediate
concerns are presented. Thirdly, space is given to develop insights which can lead to the fourth part, suggestions for further
curative educational, therapeutic and medical help. The main
task is to extend the capacity for empathy. Each participant has

to step back from their professional standpoint so that a collegial atmosphere is created. Such attempts can become pinnacles of curative education research, kindle enthusiasm and fire the flames of endurance and creativity which are needed if the educator is to create the right conditions for the therapeutic environment needed by the child.

5. Young people with special needs

Our main orientation has been towards the child. We have considered early child development and its milestones, principally the attainment of uprightness and walking, the beginning of speech and the emergence of the child's own thinking out of imitative language. Early childhood should evolve within a protected and sheltered family structure. Later the school child appears and the individual reaches out beyond the family and the life of play into the world of friendships and education. This includes the important encounter with their teacher and through this to a waking up to the world, society, history, science, art and so on. This vista of childhood takes in the period from birth to the onset of puberty.

For the child who has a special need or learning difficulty, the path towards puberty may be substantially different from the journey made by the average child. The scenery may include a period in a special school or remedial class. It may include a time in a residential school or even in a specialized hospital. They will be looked on as different even if you might wish it were not so. This is because these children *are* often substantially different from the average child, and remedial teaching, curative education and therapeutic intervention are vital factors in overcoming and learning to live with certain limitations.

Hand and eye co-ordination, allied to exact working methods, create a fine object. Restlessness is helped and self-worth enhanced.

Adolescence

Puberty has its obvious physiological consequences for the
average child as well as those with special needs. At an earlier
stage the phrase 'Puberty, Identity Seeking and Coping' was
coined to describe three phases of development specific to the
time of adolescence. If puberty is physiologically the end of
childhood, then adolescence is the beginning of inner growth
and self-awareness.

All young people have to go through a process of leaving
childhood behind and at the same time finding an increasingly
personal perspective towards their own life and life around
them. The inner situation is one of discrepancy. Childhood is
not completely left behind and at the same time adulthood is
not yet achieved. This accounts for the difficulties which often
appear in this phase of life, a main contributing factor being the
changed relationship to parents and the family home.

In all three areas of soul development, these being the life of
thought, the emotional feeling life and the area of intentionality,
significant changes take place. Youngsters begin to discover
their own thinking, even to disagree and to have their own
ideas. On an emotional level all sorts of feelings and experiences well up during this time and lead to extremes, the heights
of elation or profound melancholy. Self-criticism is a characteristic of this age, as also is the criticism which is levelled at
parents, teachers and the world in general.

It is vital that those who are to accompany the individual
with special needs out of childhood into this phase are aware of
the subtle but important changes which begin with the onset of
puberty. It is a major turning point when the young child
reveals its first experience of ego identity by saying 'I,' relating
its inner experience of self to its own body image. The time of
the seventh year and the change of teeth mark the entry into the
phase of learning proper. The ninth and tenth years are another
turning point in the experience of self-realization. All of these
changes take place during childhood whereas the entry into
puberty opens the way to a greater self-awareness on the path

of individualization. The self gradually becomes integrated into the body and this shows up in new abilities and disabilities, both personal and within relationships. Youngsters with special needs are faced with the same fundamental turning points and, according to their achievements or limitations, become youngsters who bear their legacy of early childhood experiences into the phase of adolescence.

At this point the parent or teacher can look back and ask: 'How did Peter fare with his early milestones?' 'Was he slow to walk or speak?' 'Did he say "I" in reference to himself and, if so, when?' 'Was he able to learn in school?' 'What were the things that were difficult for him?' 'Has puberty begun and how did Peter react to the change?' Obviously it is the concern of curative education to help in whichever way it can during the time of childhood but its ultimate task is to lead the child with special needs towards puberty and the encounter with adolescence. Whatever the constitution of the child up to that point it will undergo significant changes after puberty and we know that the teenage years are make or break for many such youngsters.

The background of anthroposophy helps us to realize that adulthood is attained at a much later age than we usually think. Human life is a path of becoming and adulthood is something to be attained not assumed.

Approximations on the way to adulthood

Birth
3rd Year   First 'I' experience.
7th Year   Change of teeth, beginning of learning proper.
14th Year   Puberty, entry into phase of self-recognition.
21st Year   Strengthening of ego experience. Increasing independence.
28th Year   Awakening to personal destiny and being better able to 'stand on one's own feet.'
35th Year   Entry to the main period of adult life.
42nd Year   The phase of the self-reflective ego begins. Questions of freedom and purpose become increasingly intense.

Independence and discovery

The curative educator must not ignore the future whilst having to focus so much attention on the child and its needs. Karma or destiny plays a strong part in the life of the child and this is particularly visible with a child with special needs. Many children are only partially able to wrest themselves free from some form of 'handicap' during the time up to puberty. Others will make enormous strides and be able to exercise a degree of will power and potential for change. The so-called normal person will hardly manage this degree of change over a lifetime. The purpose of curative education is to help the individual towards freedom in one form or another and this freedom is only achieved by encountering the reality and limitations of oneself as they are discovered in the way of thinking, in the emotional life or through not being able to do certain things.

Childhood is the preparation for adolescence and adulthood; the greater the degree of mastery over the hereditary and karmic limitations, the greater will be the potential for weathering the challenges and storms of adolescence. Independence has to be attained and the individual has to find out what this means. Is independence the same as egoism or is it the ability to develop, out of one's own resources, the possibility of being a useful and caring human being?

In many cases the child with special needs will have had a caring and protective family background. It is often difficult for parents to deal with the normal onset of adolescence, of evolving independence. The family and personal bonding may be so strong that the urge to protect will not allow for risk taking, resistance and the youngster's own ideas. Emotional outbursts, periods of withdrawal, awakening to sexuality and so on may well cause confusion and uncertainty in the home. In most conversations with parents of youngsters with special needs they admit that they find letting go of their adolescent youngsters extremely difficult even though they know it has to happen.

Exactness and design complexity concentrate attention and confirm a growing maturity.

Youth guidance

In recent years it has been realized that curative education has to extend into helping youngsters with special needs. The child has special needs but so has the young person. Experience with young people shows that even profoundly disturbed youngsters can reach moments of self-recognition, of an independent standpoint, through which they know what they want to do and how they want to shape their lives.

I remember a youngster with Down's syndrome who was going through adolescence. She was a lovely person and had become quite capable. In many ways she was still immature and we did not know what her future might be. From one day to the next she began to complain, to say 'I don't want to be here any more. I want to be in the new place I have just visited.' She was quite clear about this and when we told her that we thought she was right, she accepted that it would take a little time for her to be able to move on. She changed her attitude from one of complaining and instead she began to show a new quality of initiative. She stopped being a child-student and became a co-worker alongside her teachers. Through such experiences you know that curative education has reached its goal, enabling a child who may at one time have been a source of great concern to become a truly valuable member of society and a friend.

Anke Weihs, a writer and contributor to the field of youth guidance, has given a helpful image for the relationship between curative education and youth guidance. She describes a parent and child walking hand in hand beside a lake. It is a relatively peaceful scene of idealized childhood. The time comes when the parent has to let go. The child has to make its own way across the water in a small boat. It may be that the sea will be calm but at times the waves will rise and the wind will blow. For a time the boat may even disappear out of sight. The parent knows this journey has to be made. The child has to cross the lake of adolescence and encounter what will come towards them. The experiences which a child has will be its own. The hope of the parent must be that the child will reach the other side even if the child is, by then, different. Parents must want to assist their own child in leaving childhood and attaining a realistic independence as a foundation for adulthood. What is necessary, however, is for the parent to remain *with* the child, not to forget them, to love them and to carry them close to their hearts during this time of change. It could be that they or someone else will have to race across the water if the waves become too strong. Rescue attempts sometimes have to be made.[12]

This may seem to be a mere allegory but it is none the less quite a useful image to consider. The youngster with special needs has to be understood by others as has any other youngster and a particular kind of youth guidance can help them during their continuing school education leading up to graduation.

Practical aspects

How can we help the young person with special needs to weather their journey through adolescence? Firstly, it is necessary to cease regarding them as children and to change expectations. The intervention which is necessary for the child has to become a new attitude through which the youngster can begin to take responsibility for their own destiny. This is a gradual process. Consequences have to be faced. The child points a finger and cries: 'It is your fault.' The youngster has to learn to ask: 'What have I done to cause this? Why has this happened to me?'

It is helpful to change the school structure into something more like a college. Desks give way to tables. Class teachers give way to subject teachers. Science, modern history and current affairs will play a new part in the lesson contents and the student should be challenged to arrive at their own assessment, or judgment, over problems or experimental results. Education must continue to widen the student's interest in the world and extend artistic expression.

Craft work and other kinds of practical activities should play

Learning how to make useful and beautiful things.

a larger part in the education of the youngster and particularly that of the student with special needs. A new area of self-recognition can be gained in the encounter with craft and practical activities. Crafts are particularly important because through these, skill training, observation, judgments and social motivation unite in the forming of a bowl, the weaving of a basket or the dipping of a candle.

Taking responsibility for practical work is vital. To become a fellow worker alongside others in providing for the needs of others is to experience dignity and almost anyone, despite their particular limitations, can help others in some way or another. Many individuals who have been helped by curative education and youth guidance and go into work experience or enter working life, astonish the existing work force by their lack of egoism, their motivation and genuine enthusiasm to get on with the job.

Developing interest in the world, attaining social maturation and learning to work are important goals for the young person. With these the individual can go through their adolescent experiences without falling too heavily into well known negative tendencies. Sexuality which is a natural development in this time can err to the side of obsessive eroticism. The adolescent has to find a way to transform this particular emotional and physiological facet of life into the potential for a genuine love for another person.

Listening and questioning

It is perhaps apparent that youth guidance like curative education is not a technique but a practical attitude and one of the main qualities which is required is listening. Empathetic listening and a particular way of non-judgmental observing of the youngster are important attributes. Those with special needs have to set out into the risky world of today supported by the awareness and confidence of others. Life will show what might be the new possibilities for the youngster and these will be as varied as there are individuals. However, the motivation for

Everyone can do something to help make a soft toy.

change and the wish to cross new seas may not come strongly enough from youngsters themselves as they may not be able to verbalize their wishes. It is up to us to lead or even push them out of the nest of childhood. They must find their way into adolescence, be adolescent, be annoyed, moody, get into a mess and gain the kind of experiences which other adolescents go through. In this way adolescence is the narrow bridge over which every human being has to cross towards independence. One of the main deprivations of institutionalized handicapped children is to have lost out on the fulfilling experience of being a teenager in the usual sense and because of this adulthood is so difficult to achieve and so often problematic.

If a person can progress from being a child to being a truly useful and fulfilled contributor to society, sentimentality is overcome and the individual attains genuine dignity and self-respect.

The main hope is that the life experience of an adolescent
with special needs will lead them to ask questions. Identity
seeking will show up the difference between themselves and
others and particularly the normal youngster. Their childhood
friends now seem to disappear from view into employment,
higher education, travelling the world and so on. They may
appear to be caught in a kind of restricting net which they
cannot easily throw off. Youth guidance has a natural affinity
to counselling and it is important to listen to the questions of
the young person such as: Why am I handicapped? Why can't
I do what my friends do? Why can't I have a boyfriend? and so
on. Confidence and warmth from others is needed. It is well
known that in these years emotional disturbances of a severe
kind can set in as well as psychological disturbances. Many of

Keeping to the line.

From disability to community.

these appear around the middle phase of adolescence when identity seeking is at its height. Care and patience are needed in understanding, guiding and counselling at this time. Today everyone senses the presence of their limitations and in their dilemmas and questions there is little to choose between those with special needs and ourselves who are the ones who are meant to be the helpers, the educators and those who offer guidance. We need to remind ourselves of this.

Social therapy

It should be mentioned that a further and by now well developed branch has grown out from the established work of curative education. This has been termed social therapy and refers to the different kinds of working and living situations where adults of differing abilities can find meaning, dignity and a creative life style. This may be in urban group living situations where employment is found locally or in more sheltered settings where work is provided in specialized production workshops or on the land. It does not lie within the scope of this book to describe more about social therapy except to say that it is of vital importance to follow up gains made through curative education and youth guidance by helping the individual find fulfilment in adult life. One possibility for this is found in so-called independent life. Other possibilities have had to be created, especially where a sense of purpose cannot be achieved through open employment.

6. The continuing challenge

In this presentation, curative education has been put forward as a way of helping the child who we say has special needs. It is underpinned by a certain attitude discovered in its pioneers and founders, Guggenbühl, Don Bosco, Pestalozzi and others. Pioneers can be regarded as simplistic exponents of what later becomes a complex science. On the other hand founding impulses often contain the essence of what is longed for by later practitioners.

The description of child development and the examples of a number of conditions and tendencies which call for remedial intervention, the over-sensitive child, the dreamer and so on, give orientation to what we call anthroposophical curative education. In the practice of curative education it cannot be said that cures are found. It is not a matter of eradicating problems but of understanding them, helping in whatever way we can and coming to terms with the limitations of therapeutic methods. The aim of fully understanding these often puzzling conditions remains the goal of curative educational research. What is important is the realization that in the effort to understand and to try to help, our own humanity is increased and enhanced.

With this in mind we can conclude this short presentation by mentioning one of the most profound and perhaps most important issues facing curative education today. Namely, the attempt of our so-called civilized world to close the door at birth to those individuals who seek to enter life and have been discovered to be embryos which carry the genetic potential for being a child with a special need. For some reason it is possible for most of us to pass by what is taking place and not to be aware of the tragedy in our midst about which we can do so little. The bandwagon of our so-called developed, rationalized and increasingly complex world with its goal of the normal and successful creates an illusion in which the spectrum of humanity is narrowed down into certain idealized images of success and normality. Curative education works at the edges of the so-called normal spectrum knowing that every child, every human being is an expression of an eternal being seeking life with both will and purpose. Each one has a destiny, a meaning and a reason to be born. This is why we find our humanity challenged by realizing that, for instance, the prevention of Down's syndrome through genetic counselling and amniocentesis enables some parents to decide to prevent a pregnancy from achieving its full term. This has led, in one statistic, to a fifty per cent decrease in the number of Down's syndrome children being born to women over thirty-five in New York over a ten year period.

All so-called aberrations, abnormalities and other than average features have purpose and meaning for the individual and for the destiny of those they encounter. Curative education, involvement with the child with special needs makes it obvious that each one is a significant personality teaching us something which our own destiny tells us we have to learn. Curative education is about mutual help: not only the help we give the child but also the help that the child gives the parent, the teacher and the therapist.

It is perhaps good that we don't know what we have already done and are continuing to do by interfering in the destiny of so many human beings whose spirit and soul has been prepared to enter life and at the final stage is turned away. The term 'with special needs' is inadequate term for describing an intact individuality whose destiny is other than average. The conviction that karma leads individuals into specific circumstances, adequate or seemingly inadequate, presupposes that a particular life is only one in a sequence of other lives. The inadequacies, which we describe in this life have their origin in the past. They are the challenges which, if encountered and mastered, provide strength for the individual on their way into the future.

With this in mind we can be comforted by the words of Rudolf Steiner. He said that for a long time we shall be able to be happy despite knowing that other people are unhappy. This is just how life is today. But in the future it will become impossible for us to be happy whilst knowing that others are unhappy. Don Bosco responded to this realization in the help he gave to so many children. So did Albrecht Strohschein, Karl König and others. For these pioneers it was not a matter of sympathetic understanding but of doing something which would make a real difference to the present and the future of the child and young person.

Whatever your views are on the above thoughts it is a fact that looking at the world as it is, the need for curative education in one form or another is unquestionable. We may think we see a decrease in the number of children with severe developmental disabilities. We may indeed see a decline in numbers of children showing Down's syndrome, as a result of parent choice. However, these developments only belong to western Europe and North America. Don Bosco's urchins are alive today in the streets of São Paulo and Pestalozzi's refugees in Somalia and Bosnia.

In the westernized world the breakdown of secure family life, the push to high attainment in schooling, the acceptance of children's absorption in high-tech leisure pursuits and the increase in child abuse are, and will continue to be, a challenge to the educator and therapist to develop new ways to support and offer therapeutic help. We can all be involved in this if we renew our love for the child, for children; if we attempt to understand their needs through objectivity and to develop the kind of observation which can identify subtle tendencies.

In the past children who stood out from the average lived in the asylum or fell into a half-human existence. In the western world this has changed and we have described the process through which this happened. Today and in the future I believe we will come up against a different situation. It will not be the few children with special needs who will show up as different but the whole spectrum of childhood will become in need of help. The kind of assistance which will be required will be increasingly subtle and refined and the aim will be to discover an image for what we understand to be health and wholeness in the child. This will be the eventual need, to re-create society as a therapeutic environment, health giving in the widest sense. In the meantime we should take each child or young person as we meet them and help them to shine with the colour of their destiny. In the words of Karl König:

> The curative educational attitude comes about where a new kind of humanity begins to grow in the heart. Then everyone with a human countenance is seen as a brother and sister. It is a humility so undaunted and yet so tender that when confronting need, degradation and suffering, it will bring those tears to the eyes which will make our will to help strong and devoted, and ready for decision.[13]

Karl König with a young friend.

Photographic acknowledgments

Barnados (p.26); Paul Bock (pp.34, 37, 51, 52, 54, 67, 69, 80, 89); Hulton Deutsch Collection Limited (pp.23); Syl Edgerley (pp.62, 63, 74, 82); Werner Groth (p.37); Stephen Hopewell (p.32); Cornelius Pietzner (pp.15, 78); Nick Poole (pp.58, 65, 96, 98, 99, 101); Caren Simon (pp.76, 100); Margriet Stujit (pp. 43, 93); The Wellcome Trust (pp.20, 21); Paul White Photography (p.75).

References

1. Rudolf Steiner, *Curative Education,* lectures of 1924, Rudolf Steiner Press, Bristol 1993.
2. Karl König, *Being Human,* Anthroposophic Press.
3. *Special Educational Needs,* (Warnock Report), HMSO, London 1978.
4. Rudolf Steiner, *The Course of my Life,* Anthroposophic Press.
5. Karl König, 'Mignon; A tentative history of curative education,' *The Cresset* (Journal of the Camphill Movement) 1960.
6. Thomas Weihs, 'Don Bosco,' *The Cresset* (Journal of the Camphill Movement) 1956.
7. Thomas Weihs, 'Thomas Barnardo,' *The Cresset* (Journal of the Camphill Movement) 1955.
8. Albrecht Strohschein 'The Beginning of Curative Education,' in *Curative Education,* Rudolf Steiner Press, Bristol, 1993.
9. From Steven Schwartz and James H. Johnson, *Psychopathology of Childhood,* Pergamon.
10. Bruno Bettelheim, *The Empty Fortress,* Free Press, USA.
11. Lotte Sahlmann, 'Constitutional Over-Sensitivity,' *The Cresset* (Journal of the Camphill Movement) 1972.
12. Anke Weihs, *Camphill Working Papers Vol. 1,* Camphill Press, 1994
13. Karl König, 'The Meaning and Value of Curative Education and Work,' *The Cresset* (Journal of the Camphill Movement) 1965.

Further reading

Barron, Judy & Sean, *There's a boy in here*, Chapman 1993.

Carlgren, F., *Education Towards Freedom*, Lanthorn Press.

Childs, Gilbert, *Steiner Education*, Floris Books, 1992.

Clarke, P., Kofsky, H., Lauruol, J., *To a Different Drumbeat*, Hawthorn Press.

Erikson, Eric H., *Identity: Youth and Crisis*, Faber & Faber.

Glas, Norbert, *Conception, Birth and Early Childhood*, Anthroposophic Press.

Hansmann, Henning, *Education for Special Needs*, Floris Books, 1992.

Harwood, A.C., *The Way of a Child*, Anthroposophic Press.

Heydebrand, Caroline von, *Childhood: The Growing Soul*, Anthroposophic Press.

Holtzapfel, Walter, *Children's Destinies*, Mercury Press.

Hunt, Nigel, *The World of Nigel Hunt, The Diary of a Down's Syndrome Youth*, Kennedy-Galton Centre for Mental Retardation Research, Harperbury Hospital, 1966.

Koepke, Herman, *Encountering the Self: Transformation and Destiny in the Ninth Year*, Anthroposophic Press.

König, Karl, *The First Three Years of a Child*, Floris Books, 1984.

Lievegoed, Bernard, *Phases of Childhood*, Floris Books, 1987.

Pietzner, Carlo, *Questions of Destiny*, Anthroposophic Press.

Portman, Neil, *The Disappearance of Childhood (How TV is Changing Children's Lives)*, Comet.

Weihs, Thomas J., *Children in Need of Special Care*, Souvenir Press.

Weihs, Thomas J., *Embryogenesis*, Floris Books, 1986.

Williams, Donna, *Nobody Nowhere*, Corgi 1993.

Index

Figures in italics refer to illustrations